D1226304

INTRODUCING
ISSUES WITH
OPPOSING
VIEWPOINTS®

Human Rights

Lauri S. Scherer, *Book Editor*

GREENHAVEN PRESS
A part of Gale, Cengage Learning

GALE
CENGAGE Learning·

Detroit • New York • San Francisco • New Haven, Conn • Waterville, Maine • London

Elizabeth Des Chenes, *Director, Content Strategy*
Cynthia Sanner, *Publisher*
Douglas Dentino, *Manager, New Product*

© 2014 Greenhaven Press, a part of Gale, Cengage Learning

WCN: 01-100-101

LIBRARY OF CONGRESS CATALOGING-IN-PUBLICATION DATA

Human Rights / Lauri S. Scherer, book editor.
    pages cm. -- (Introducing issues with opposing viewpoints)
    Summary: "Introducing Issues with Opposing Viewpoints: Human Rights: Introducing Issues with Opposing Viewpoints is a series that examines current issues from different viewpoints, set up in a pro/con format"-- Provided by publisher.
    Includes bibliographical references and index.
    ISBN 978-0-7377-6924-1 (hardback)
    1. Human rights. 2. Human rights--United States I. Scherer, Lauri S., editor of compilation.
    JC571.H76845 2014
    323--dc23
                                                                    2013029611

Printed in the United States of America
1 2 3 4 5 6 7 18 17 16 15 14

Contents

Chapter 3: How Should the United States Protect Human Rights?

Foreword

Indulging in a wide spectrum of ideas, beliefs, and perspectives is a critical cornerstone of democracy. After all, it is often debates over differences of opinion, such as whether to legalize abortion, how to treat prisoners, or when to enact the death penalty, that shape our society and drive it forward. Such diversity of thought is frequently regarded as the hallmark of a healthy and civilized culture. As the Reverend Clifford Schutjer of the First Congregational Church in Mansfield, Ohio, declared in a 2001 sermon, "Surrounding oneself with only like-minded people, restricting what we listen to or read only to what we find agreeable is irresponsible. Refusing to entertain doubts once we make up our minds is a subtle but deadly form of arrogance." With this advice in mind, Introducing Issues with Opposing Viewpoints books aim to open readers' minds to the critically divergent views that comprise our world's most important debates.

Introducing Issues with Opposing Viewpoints simplifies for students the enormous and often overwhelming mass of material now available via print and electronic media. Collected in every volume is an array of opinions that captures the essence of a particular controversy or topic. Introducing Issues with Opposing Viewpoints books embody the spirit of nineteenth-century journalist Charles A. Dana's axiom: "Fight for your opinions, but do not believe that they contain the whole truth, or the only truth." Absorbing such contrasting opinions teaches students to analyze the strength of an argument and compare it to its opposition. From this process readers can inform and strengthen their own opinions, or be exposed to new information that will change their minds. Introducing Issues with Opposing Viewpoints is a mosaic of different voices. The authors are statesmen, pundits, academics, journalists, corporations, and ordinary people who have felt compelled to share their experiences and ideas in a public forum. Their words have been collected from newspapers, journals, books, speeches, interviews, and the Internet, the fastest growing body of opinionated material in the world.

Introducing Issues with Opposing Viewpoints shares many of the well-known features of its critically acclaimed parent series, Opposing Viewpoints. The articles are presented in a pro/con format, allowing readers to absorb divergent perspectives side by side. Active reading questions preface each viewpoint, requiring the student to approach the material thoughtfully and carefully. Useful charts, graphs, and cartoons supplement each article. A thorough introduction provides readers with crucial background on an issue. An annotated bibliography points the reader toward articles, books, and websites that contain additional information on the topic. An appendix of organizations to contact contains a wide variety of charities, nonprofit organizations, political groups, and private enterprises that each hold a position on the issue at hand. Finally, a comprehensive index allows readers to locate content quickly and efficiently.

Introducing Issues with Opposing Viewpoints is also significantly different from Opposing Viewpoints. As the series title implies, its presentation will help introduce students to the concept of opposing viewpoints and learn to use this material to aid in critical writing and debate. The series' four-color, accessible format makes the books attractive and inviting to readers of all levels. In addition, each viewpoint has been carefully edited to maximize a reader's understanding of the content. Short but thorough viewpoints capture the essence of an argument. A substantial, thought-provoking essay question placed at the end of each viewpoint asks the student to further investigate the issues raised in the viewpoint, compare and contrast two authors' arguments, or consider how one might go about forming an opinion on the topic at hand. Each viewpoint contains sidebars that include at-a-glance information and handy statistics. A Facts About section located in the back of the book further supplies students with relevant facts and figures.

Following in the tradition of the Opposing Viewpoints series, Greenhaven Press continues to provide readers with invaluable exposure to the controversial issues that shape our world. As John Stuart Mill once wrote: "The only way in which a human being can make some approach to knowing the whole of a subject is by hearing what can be said about it by persons of every variety of opinion and studying all modes in which it can be looked at by every character of mind. No wise man ever acquired his wisdom in any mode but this." It is to this principle that Introducing Issues with Opposing Viewpoints books are dedicated.

Introduction

The United States has long been looked to as the world's leader, and even enforcer, of human rights. Its reputation as a human rights beacon developed as World War II ended, when it was globally revered for liberating Europe from Adolf Hitler's Nazi German regime, one of history's most egregious human rights violators. America's standing as a guardian of human rights was solidified over later decades as it became engaged in the Cold War, a multidecade ideological conflict with the Communist Soviet Union (present-day Russia) for power and influence around the globe. In the ideological standoff between the two superpowers, the United States represented freedom, democracy, and opportunity, which appealed to citizens of almost every country on earth. This, coupled with its reputation for being a stalwart defender of its own citizens' rights to freedom of speech, religion, and other rights, made the United States unquestionably the world's human rights leader of the twentieth century.

But in the twenty-first century, the United States has faced new challenges and enemies that have tested both its resolve and reputation as this leader. The war on terror—which officially began following the terrorist attacks of September 11, 2001, in which nearly three thousand Americans were killed when terrorists crashed airliners into important buildings—gave rise to new, challenging scenarios to which the United States has struggled to respond in a way that both protects its security and champions human rights.

For example, early in the war on terror, to debrief suspected enemies about potential terrorist plans, the administration of President George W. Bush approved the use of harsh interrogation tactics—some of which bordered on human rights violations. The most famous of these was waterboarding, a process in which interrogators make a suspect feel as if he is drowning by restraining him and either immersing his head in water or leaning him backward and pouring water over his towel-covered face. Subjects feel intense panic and anxiety and typically cannot withstand more than even a few seconds of such treatment.

Waterboarding became a highly controversial interrogation technique. Opponents argued that it amounted to torture and violated both US and international human rights standards. Proponents argued that it was legally consistent with human rights declarations and was a valid technique given the context of fighting people who target innocent civilians as their main battle method. The American public was clearly torn on the topic: One 2009 poll found that 60 percent of Americans considered waterboarding to be torture, yet another poll the same year revealed that almost the same number—55 percent—thought it was justified if it helped suspected terrorists give up plots to kill innocent Americans. In other words, Americans seemed to think the threats they faced justified using torture and violating the human rights of those intent on killing them.

As the war on terror continued into a new president's administration, waterboarding eventually became viewed as inconsistent with the US commitment to human rights and as even undermining the war on terror itself. It was thus abandoned as an interrogation technique by President Barack Obama in the first year of his presidency. "I believe that waterboarding was torture and, whatever legal rationales were used, it was a mistake," he said in 2009, adding that any use of torture "corrodes the character of a country."[1]

Yet the Obama administration pursued other tactics in the war on terror that attracted equal scrutiny as possible violations of human rights. For example, Obama greatly expanded the use of drone warfare. Drones are unmanned combat weapons that are operated by remote control. They are increasingly used by the US military because they keep soldiers out of ground combat and can make war more precise and less deadly for both the military and innocent bystanders. Supporters say drones' reduced collateral damage makes them an effective, efficient, and humane weapon. Opponents, however, argue that because they are machines, drones kill indiscriminately—they cannot tell adults from children or enemies from innocents and as a result, kill innocent men, women, and children in a way that violates international human rights.

Although drones were first used under Bush, Obama greatly expanded their scope. According to CNN, Obama authorized six times the number of drone strikes in his first four years of office than Bush did in his eight years in office. Even more controversially, Obama occasionally used drones to target American citizens who are suspected terrorists. For example, in September 2011 the US military killed Anwar al-Awlaki, an American of Yemeni descent. Alhough he was affiliated with al Qaeda terrorist network and was allegedly involved in numerous terrorist attacks and plots, his status as an American citizen made his assassination a tricky legal issue. Critics say he should have been extradited to the United States and afforded due process, the constitutional right of every American to receive a fair trial, and other legal rights. "Al-Awlaki was born here, he's an American citizen, he was never tried or charged for any crimes," said US congressman Ron Paul. "To start assassinating American citizens without charges—we should think very seriously about this,"[2] he warned. Yet the Obama administration and others justified Awlaki's killing by saying that extradition would have been impossible, that other legal steps were taken to make the assassination lawful, and that his known involvement in terrorist activities made him a treasonous enemy of the state. As US representative Peter King put it, "It was entirely legal. If a citizen takes up arms against his own country, he becomes an enemy of the country,"[3] thus forfeiting the rights afforded to citizens.

Given these controversies, many wonder whether the United States can continue to credibly lead the world in human rights. As activist Michael Payne put it, "Mr. Obama need not lecture [other world leaders] about human rights. He needs to look inward, search his own conscience, and clearly understand how his decisions and actions are violating the human rights of many thousands of people in other sovereign nations."[4] Yet others argue that no nation has a perfect human rights record and that the United States remains alone among nations in its commitment to so many different kinds of rights in so many different places. Even more importantly, as American power and influence fade and the power and influence of other countries rise, none has proven so dedicated to uncovering human rights abuses or preventing them as has the United States. "It turns out the alternative to American leadership is no leadership at all, or not much of one," writes world affairs columnist Frida Ghitis. "The powers whose rise has paralleled the American decline, such as China, have shown no inclination to lift a finger in defense of human rights or for the prevention of conflicts that could devastate civilian populations."[5]

What human rights the United States in the twenty-first century should seek to protect is among the numerous issues explored in *Introducing Issues with Opposing Viewpoints: Human Rights*. In addition to considering what human rights protections the United States should enforce, viewpoints will also debate what constitutes a human right and a human rights violation. Thought-provoking article pairs and essay prompts, as well as helpful appendixes, encourage readers to examine the issues more deeply and form their own opinions on the topic.

Notes

1. Quoted in Ewan MacAskill, "Obama: 'I Believe Waterboarding Was Torture, and It Was a Mistake,'" *Guardian* (Manchester, UK), April 29, 2009. www.guardian.co.uk/world/2009/apr/30/obama -waterboarding-mistake.
2. Quoted in Michelle Martinez, "US Drone Killing of American al-Awlaki Prompts Legal, Moral Debate," CNN.com, September 30, 2011. http://articles.cnn.com/2011-09-30/politics/politics_tar geting-us-citizens_1_al-awlaki-yemeni-embassy-drone-missile? _s=PM:POLITICS.
3. Quoted in Martinez, "US Drone Killing of American al-Awlaki Prompts Legal, Moral Debate."
4. Michael Payne, "What Audacity! President Obama Lectures China on Human Rights," OpEdNews, January 22, 2011. www .opednews.com/articles/What-Audacity-President-O-by-michael -payne-110121-900.html.
5. Frida Ghitis, "On Human Rights, US Must Lead—or No One Will," *Miami (FL) Herald,* August 6, 2012. www.miamiherald .com/2012/08/06/2930361/on-human-rights-us-must-lead-or .html.

Chapter 1

What Constitutes a Human Right?

A protester rallies against the US National Security Agency's violations of the right to privacy.

Internet Access Is a Human Right

"In this modern, networked world, we must ensure the right to free expression is as protected online as [it is] offline."

Chris Coons

Chris Coons is a Democratic US senator from Delaware. In the following viewpoint he argues that Internet access is a fundamental human right. He explains that the Internet is the modern-day public square— it is where people gather to discuss new ideas, criticize the government, debate religious ideas, and exercise other forms of free speech. Just as free speech is considered a human right offline, Coons argues, it must be considered a human right online, too. For all of these reasons, he contends, the world should view Internet access as a human right and defend and promote it the way it does other human rights.

AS YOU READ, CONSIDER THE FOLLOWING QUESTIONS:

1. In which nations is Internet access severely restricted, according to Coons?
2. Where does the author say the Internet has been used as a tool of liberation?
3. What investment does Coons say the United States made in 2008 to protect and promote Internet freedom?

Sometimes it's called "information security." Other times, it's called "Internet management," or a "hate-free Internet." Whatever the code-name for it, too many foreign governments, including Syria, Iran and China, restrict Internet as a tool for suppressing free speech, free assembly and a free press.

Though the United States has invested tens of millions of dollars in defending Internet freedom around the world in recent years—including by equipping censored populations with technologies to evade digital repression—we can and must do more to ensure Internet freedom remains a fundamental tenet of U.S. foreign policy.

With nearly one-third of mankind—some two billion people—now online, the Internet has clearly become the public square of the 21st century. It is where ideas are exchanged, viewpoints are debated,

Many think having access to the Internet is a human right because the Internet functions as a modern-day town square, where people "gather" to discuss new ideas, criticize the government, debate religious ideas, and engage in other forms of free speech.

and commerce takes place, and in this modern, networked world, we must ensure the right to free expression is as protected online as [it is] offline.

There is deep bipartisan support in Congress for robust U.S. engagement to secure digital freedom around the world. In fact, the Senate Global Internet Freedom Caucus, led by Senators Mark Kirk (R-Ill.), Bob Casey (D-Pa.) and myself, and the House Global Internet Freedom Caucus, led by Representative Chris Smith (R-N.J.) are teaming up today [May 10, 2012,] with the Center for a New American Security for a discussion of U.S. policy to promote Internet freedom globally.

The Internet can be used as a tool of liberation, as we saw in revolutions that swept the Arab world last spring, or of repression, as we continue to witness in places such as Iran and China. Popular movements and entrenched governments both clearly see how the unique power of the Internet can spread democratic ideas and demands for human rights and basic freedoms.

These fundamental values, which should be granted to citizens around the world as enshrined in the Universal Declaration of Human Rights, are central to who we are as Americans.

We must continue to pursue an American foreign policy that protects the "right to connect" as a U.S. foreign policy priority. The Senate Global Internet Freedom Caucus advocates for the promotion of policies that promotes rights of all people to use the Internet and other forms of technology to exercise basic freedoms globally. In order to achieve this goal, we must engage with governments, individuals, and the private sector to preserve the Internet as an open platform for commerce and communication.

Led by Secretary of State Hillary Clinton [2009–2013], this [Barack Obama] administration has recognized the "right to connect" as a fundamental human right, and the American people have already made a significant investment of more than $70 million since 2008

in protecting and promoting Internet freedom globally. This funding has supported a number of projects, including the development of censorship-circumvention technology, cyber self-defense training, and equipping people to evade repression.

Despite remarkable innovations in technology, there is more work to be done, as restrictions to Internet access and online censorship, manipulation, and monitoring continue to rise around the world. U.S. global leadership is critical if we are to make progress in this area, and we cannot be hampered by the false perception that global Internet freedom is at odds with domestic cyber security measures and the protection of intellectual property. In fact, these policies can and should complement each other. We can implement vigorous standards to protect intellectual property and network security while still wholeheartedly supporting Internet freedom globally.

Internet freedom—the freedom to exchange thought, opinion, expression, and association to meet political, social, education, or religious objectives—should not be restricted for law-abiding citizens in the United States or anywhere in the world. Advancing this right in repressive regimes across the globe must be a fundamental tenet of our foreign policy in the 21st century. As with all great moral challenges we face as an international community, continued American leadership and engagement is essential if we are to succeed.

EVALUATING THE AUTHOR'S ARGUMENTS:

Chris Coons, the author of this viewpoint, is a US senator. Vinton Cerf, the author of the following viewpoint, is a computer scientist and a founder of the Internet. How does knowing these authors' backgrounds influence your opinion of their arguments? Are you more or less inclined to agree with one over the other? Why or why not?

Internet Access Is Not a Human Right

Vinton Cerf, as told to Brooke Gladstone

"While the Internet is a terrific tool for improving the human condition, it does not rise to the level of a human right."

In the following viewpoint Vinton Cerf argues that Internet access is not a human right. He acknowledges that the Internet is very important for promoting free speech, which is a human right. But he cautions against confusing the technology (the Internet) with the right (free speech). He says technology changes too fast to be considered a human right in and of itself; human rights are more permanent concepts, such as the right to life and freedom. Furthermore, rights are things that can be offered equally to everyone—Cerf points out that labeling Internet access a human right requires that it be available to everyone, which means requiring governments to give their citizens Internet access, computers, and networks. In his opinion, this is problematic. He concludes that a distinction must be made between the Internet and what the Internet is used for. On these grounds, he opposes the viewpoint that Internet access is a human right.

Cerf is a computer scientist who helped found the Internet. Brook Gladstone is host and managing editor of National Public Radio's *On the Media* program.

AS YOU READ, CONSIDER THE FOLLOWING QUESTIONS:
1. How does Cerf say he would respond if someone asked him whether he had a human right to access a horse?
2. What does the author say are "almost immutable"?
3. Whose responsibility is it to support human rights online, according to Cerf?

*B*rooke Gladstone: We all cry foul when access to the Web is threatened or cut off altogether, as it was in Egypt during the protests there, exactly one year ago [in January 2011]. Last summer, a United Nations report declared that the Internet had become, quote, "An indispensable tool for realizing a range of human rights." Some countries have gone as far as calling access to the Internet itself a human right. Not so fast, says Vinton Cerf, one of the true founders of the Internet. In a recent New York Times op-ed, he argues that while the Internet is a terrific tool for improving the human condition, it does not rise to the level of a human right.

Vinton Cerf: Today if someone said, well you still have a human right to access to a horse, my reaction would be, well, first I don't know where I'd put it, and second, I have 250 horses sitting in my garage right now, which is—you know, the replacement for the barn. And I don't need the other one. So I—my only concern here is not to get so tangled up in a particular technology that we lose sight of the intent, which is to assure the human right to communicate.

Believe me, I am the last person in the world to argue that Internet is not useful. It is incredibly useful. It is incredibly powerful. . . .

You wrote that however well meaning the argument is for declaring Internet access a right that the status demands a higher bar and that if we lower it, we could end up valuing the wrong things. Like what? What's the real danger here?

If you look in the Constitution, if you look at the United Nations Declaration of Human Rights, you find that these rights are often associated with things like the right to speak, the right to hear, the right to assemble, the right to food and shelter and clothing. These are very fundamental, and they are, I would say, almost immutable, whereas the technologies that enable them are going to change over time.

Internet Access Around the World

Internet access varies greatly around the world. Although the Internet plays an important role, some argue that requiring governments to provide access to it is problematic and confuses the essence of human rights.

World Internet Penetration Rates by Geographic Regions

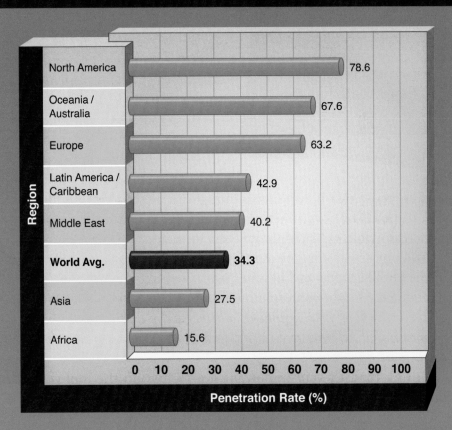

Taken from: Internet World Stats. www.internetworldstats.com/stats.htm. Penetration rates are based on a world population of 7,017,846,922 and 2,405,518,376 estimated Internet users on June 20, 2012.

And so, my alarm here was that binding a particular technology to human rights seems like it has the potential mistake that after you've done this and the technology changes then you have to say, oh well, we didn't really mean that. This new technology is our new human right.

But why can't that right transfer from technology to technology?

If you were to take the view that the Internet is a human right or access to the Internet is a human right, the implication of that is that everyone in the world should be given access, that it has to be provided by the society. And here we run into a problem. We might have as a goal that everyone should have access, and we might even take the view that you can't be denied access when it's available.

The problem is requiring it to be available. And, and I think that's where I have a problem.

If we agree for the purposes of this conversation that Internet access does not rise to the level of a human right, do you think it rises to the level of a civil right? Or can you find some analogy in American history to address that?

The 1934 Telecommunications Act, which, by the way, also included the accessibility to electrical power, comes very close because those two utilities were thought to be sufficiently important that it should be government policy to make it feasible for anyone to have reasonable expectation of access to them.

And one could imagine that the present day broadband initiatives in the United States and in other countries, like Australia, rise to the level of a civil right conferred by intent by the government.

The bedrock of your argument, whether we're talking about horses or phones, is that Internet access is always a tool for obtaining something else that's more important.

I think that it's very important not to mix up the tool with the outcome. The outcome is the ability to communicate—to speak, to

Cofounder of the Internet Vinton Cerf (shown) believes that technology like that used for the Internet changes too fast to be considered a human right in itself.

hear, to gain access to information. But there might someday be other technologies that enable these outcomes even more effectively, and we'd want to adopt those as alternatives.

You conclude your op-ed by asserting that the most fundamental issue here is the responsibility of the technology creators themselves to support human and civil rights. Google, along with the Yahoo! and Microsoft, has in the past censored search results when asked to do it by the Chinese Government.

I know Google has since changed its policy on this. Cisco and others have sold tools to repressive regimes that enable them to target oppressed groups, like the Chinese can target the [suppressed spiritual group] Falun Gong. This would be a failure to ensure that the Internet remains a means to a better life, wouldn't it?

Yeah, I think it is a more nuanced question than that. This is a two-edged sword. The things that we might do in the Internet to protect people from abuse might also be used by others to inhibit speech.

And it would be healthy, I think, for engineers like me and others to be reminded that these technologies are important tools in the context of exercising civil rights or even human rights, and that we should be alert to things that we can do to assure that they can continue to be used that way.

EVALUATING THE AUTHOR'S ARGUMENTS:

Vinton Cerf argues that the best way to promote human rights online is not to make Internet access a human right but rather to make sure technology is used for positive and productive purposes. To this end, he thinks technology companies should refuse to comply with governments that censor or use technology to repress people. What is your opinion of this suggestion? Is promoting human rights as important, more important, or less important than making Internet access a human right? Explain your answer.

Access to Water Is a Human Right

Pablo Solón

"The right to drinking water and sanitation is a human right that is essential."

Access to clean, potable water is a human right, argues Pablo Solón in the following viewpoint taken from a speech to the United Nations General Assembly. Solón contends that water is critical to human life, that without clean water people succumb to numerous diseases, and if they survive, their quality of life is drastically reduced. Because water is essential to life, Solón maintains that access to it a human right. He explains that numerous organizations and conventions have listed sanitation and health as crucial to human dignity and that clean water is key to affording both of those. Solón concludes that lack of access to clean water is a global crisis, one that can be righted by recognizing access to clean water as a human right and protecting and defending it.

Solón is Bolivia's ambassador to the United Nations.

Allow me to begin the presentation of this resolution by recalling that human beings are essentially water. About two thirds of our organism is comprised of water. Some 75% of our brain is made up of water, and water is the principal vehicle for the electrochemical transmissions of our body.

Water Is Life

Our blood flows like a network of rivers in our body. Blood helps transport nutrients and energy to our organism. Water also carries from our cells waste products for excretion. Water helps to regulate the temperature of our body.

The loss of 20% of body water can cause death. It is possible to survive for weeks without food, but it is not possible to survive more than a few days without water. Water is life.

That is why, today, we present this historic resolution for the consideration of the plenary of the [United Nations (UN)] General Assembly.

The right to health was originally recognised in 1946 by the World Health Organisation. In 1948, the Universal Declaration of Human Rights declared, among other rights, "the right to life", "the right to education", and "the right to work".

In 1966 these were furthered in the International Covenant on Economic, Social and Cultural rights with the recognition of "the right to social security", and "the right to an adequate standard of living", including adequate food, clothing and adequate shelter.

However, the human right to water has continued [to] not be fully recognised, despite clear references in various international legal instruments such as: the Convention on the Elimination of All forms of Racial Discrimination, the Convention on the Elimination of All

Forms of Discrimination Against Women, the Convention on the Rights of the Child, and the Convention on the Rights of Persons with Disabilities.

The Human Right to Water

This is why we, the co-sponsors, present this resolution in order that we now recognise the human right to water and sanitation, at a time when illness caused by lack of drinking water and sanitation causes more deaths than does war.

- Every year, 3.5 million people die of waterborne illness.
- Diarrhoea is the second largest cause of death among children under five. The lack of access to potable water kills more children than AIDS, malaria and smallpox combined.
- Worldwide, about one in eight people lack potable water.
- In just one day, more than 200 million hours of women's time is consumed by collecting and transporting water for domestic use.
- The lack of sanitation is far worse, for it affects 2.6 billion people, or 40% of the global population.

These Tanzanians enjoy recently improved access to freshwater. Because water is essential to life, many feel access to water is a basic human right.

According to the report on sanitation by the [UN] independent expert: "Sanitation, more than many other human rights issues, evokes the concept of human dignity. Consider the vulnerability and shame that so many people experience every day when, again, they are forced to defecate in the open, in a bucket or a plastic bag."

The vast majority of illnesses around the world are caused by fecal matter. It is estimated that sanitation could reduce child death due to diarrhoea by more than one third.

On any given day, half all hospital beds are occupied by patients suffering from illnesses associated with lack of access to safe water and lack of sanitation.

Getting Closer to Human Dignity

Human rights were not born as fully developed concepts, but are built on reality and experience. For example, the human rights to education and work included in the Universal Declaration on Human Rights were constructed and specified over time, with the International Covenant on Economic, Social and Cultural Rights and other international legal instruments such as the Declaration on the Rights of Indigenous Peoples. The same will occur with the human right to water and sanitation.

That is why we emphasise and encourage in the third operative paragraph of this resolution that the independent expert continue working on all aspects of her mandate and present to the General Assembly "the principal challenges related to the realisation of the human right to safe and clean drinking water and sanitation and their impact on the achievement of Millennium Development Goals".

The Summit on the Millennium Development Goals is approaching, and it is necessary to give a clear signal to the world that drinking-water and sanitation are a human right, and that we will do everything pos-

Lack of Clean Water Causes Disease

Lack of clean water is a critical problem in some parts of the world, in part because it spreads disease. This map shows the percentage of total disease burden caused by unsafe or unclean water, by country.

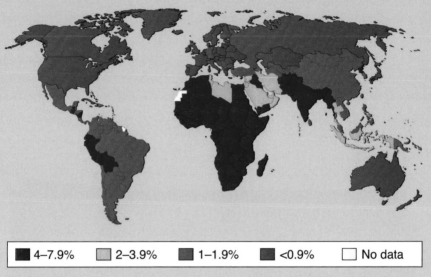

| ■ 4–7.9% | ▨ 2–3.9% | ■ 1–1.9% | ■ <0.9% | ☐ No data |

Taken from: Nature.com.

sible to reach this goal, which we have only five more years [by 2015] to achieve.

That is why we are convinced of the importance of the second operative paragraph of this resolution, which "calls upon states and international organisations to provide financial resources, capacity-building and technology transfer, through international assistance and cooperation, in particular to developing countries, in order to scale up efforts to provide safe, clean, accessible and affordable drinking water and sanitation for all."

Life's Essentials Are Rights

The right to drinking water and sanitation is a human right that is essential for the full enjoyment of life.

Drinking water and sanitation are not only elements or principal components of other rights such as "the right to an adequate standard of living". The right to drinking water and sanitation are independent rights that should be recognised as such. It is not enough to urge states to comply with their human rights obligations relative to access to drinking water and sanitation. Instead, it is necessary to call on states to promote and protect the human right to drinking water and sanitation.

Before moving to the consideration of this resolution, I would like to ask all delegations to bear in mind the fact that, according to the 2009 report of the World Health Organisation and UNICEF [United Nations Children's Fund] entitled "Diarrhoea: Why children are still dying and what can be done", 24,000 children die in developing countries every day from preventable causes like diarrhoea contracted from unclean water. That is one child death every three and a half seconds.

One, two, three . . .

As my people say: "Now is the time."

EVALUATING THE AUTHOR'S ARGUMENTS:

Pablo Solón quotes from several sources to support the points he makes in his viewpoint. Make a list of everyone he quotes, including their credentials and the nature of their comments. Then analyze his sources—are they credible? Are they well-qualified to speak on this subject? What specific points do they support?

Access to Water Is Not a Human Right

Jacob Mchangama

"Declaring water and sanitation as human rights constitutes a threat to both international law and the poor themselves."

In the following viewpoint Jacob Mchangama argues that access to water should not be considered a human right. He acknowledges that water access is a critical problem but warns that declaring water a human right threatens to make the problem worse. This is because human rights are a government's responsibility to provide and protect; governments are responsible for guaranteeing their citizens the right to liberty, the right to free speech, or the right to assemble, for example. Should governments begin to control the granting of water rights, he warns, they could too easily use their power to deny access to water to certain segments of the population. Furthermore, declaring water a human right suggests an expectation for developed countries (such as the United States) to help developing nations (such as Bolivia) deliver it—but such an arrangement would ignore many of the ways in which developing nations violate other human rights in ways that cause the lack of access to water. Mchangama concludes that the instinct to declare water a human right is well-meaning, but in reality it could have disastrous consequences for the world's most vulnerable peoples.

Mchangama is head of legal affairs at the Danish think tank CEPOS and lectures on international human rights at the University of Copenhagen.

AS YOU READ, CONSIDER THE FOLLOWING QUESTIONS:
1. What is the difference between positive and negative rights, according to Mchangama?
2. How might dictators abuse people if water were to become a human right, according to the author?
3. Who is John Sammis, according to Mchangama?

Considering that 2.5 billion people lack sanitation and 900 million people are without access to safe drinking water, last week's [late July 2010] United Nations [UN] General Assembly resolution on water might seem like a welcome development. But declaring water and sanitation as human rights constitutes a threat to both international law and the poor themselves.

Human Rights Must Be Clear and Definable

In international law, individually enforceable human rights are things the state cannot take away from you—life, liberty, property—not things that the state must provide for you with taxpayer money. More importantly, this declaration will not help those whose health and quality of life are threatened by the lack of clean water and sanitation.

> ## FAST FACT
>
> In Punjab, India, efforts to provide free water to villagers have overtaxed the area's groundwater. Groundwater levels are dropping up to two feet per year, according to the National Geophysical Research Institute, which predicts imminent water shortages for Punjab's 114 million residents.

For rights to have meaning, it must be clear what they are and who is responsible for upholding them. Take free speech: If a government arrests a dissident for peaceful statements or thoughts, it is breaching its obligation to uphold a clear human right. Courts would then be responsible for upholding this right.

Water Depends on Things Not Related to Rights

The right to clean water and sanitation is far less definable and depends on economic development, technology and infrastructure. Above all, if people have a right to water and sanitation, other people must provide it—in practice, governments using public money. Such privileges are called "positive rights," as opposed to "negative rights" that cannot be taken away from you. So this is really a call for state intervention, at the expense of other priorities and freedoms—and water is no more a practically enforceable human right than other essential commodities, such as food, clothing or shelter.

This resolution follows naturally from activists' ideological resistance to the privatization of water. This ignores the countless examples, from Bolivia to Egypt, where governments have failed to provide clean water due to corruption, cronyism, mismanagement and waste. It also ignores successful private models in Bolivia, Chile, Denmark

The author warns that government control over water access is dangerous, as it could deny such access to certain segments of governments' populations.

After twenty years of working to improve people's access to clean water and sanitation, many more of the world's people had access to drinking water in 2010 than in 1990.

Population with access to drinking water in the world in 1990–2010

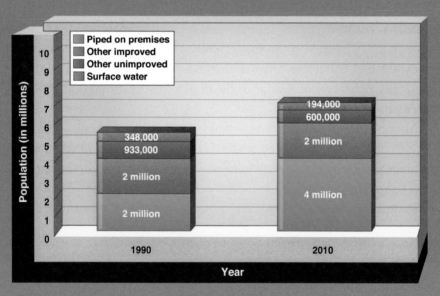

Taken from: World Health Organization/UNICEF Joint Monitoring Programme (JMP) for Water Supply and Saturation, 2012.

and elsewhere. Giving governments ultimate control over the supply of water may even be dangerous, because authoritarian regimes can use their power to punish the recalcitrant and reward their supporters.

Developing Real Rights

The resolution also devalues true human rights. By demanding that developed countries "provide financial resources and technology transfer" to developing countries, the resolution implies that the rich are violating the human rights of people without water in poor countries. This allows many countries, such as the proposer, Bolivia, to deflect criticism away from their own real rights violations—arbitrary detentions, corruption, censorship—while portraying themselves as victims of the West.

So far, defenders of traditional human rights have been reluctant to criticize this political agenda. No one wants to be perceived as being against clean water and human rights. So democratic countries such as Italy, Germany, Spain and Norway voted for the resolution with Egypt, China, Pakistan and Cuba, which deny human rights to their citizens, while 41 countries abstained, including Canada, the United States, Australia and Britain. No country had the courage to reject it, leaving the way open for the adoption of a legally binding protocol.

Water Is the Wrong Right

Those who are against the idea, such as the United States, hope this non-binding resolution will not matter because "the legal implications of a declared right to water had not yet been fully considered," as U.S. diplomat John Sammis told delegates. Such procedural theory ignores the political reality of governments' gaining greater power over their citizens' lives, particularly in poor countries where oppressive economic regimes are supported by Western charities and activists.

If democratic states abandon the freedoms of true human rights, they abandon the poor to many more decades of state-imposed poverty, corruption and inefficiency.

EVALUATING THE AUTHOR'S ARGUMENTS:

Jacob Mchangama and Pablo Solón (author of the previous viewpoint) disagree on whether access to water is a human right. After reading both viewpoints, with which author do you agree? In your answer, cite a particular piece of evidence or argument that swayed you.

Health Care Is a Human Right

Robert Greenberg

"Health care as a human right occupies a firm position."

Robert Greenberg is professor emeritus of pediatrics at the University of New Mexico School of Medicine. In the following viewpoint he argues that health care should be a universal human right. He explains that it is decent, moral, and proper to give sick, suffering people care when they need it, even if they cannot afford to pay for it. The opposite scenario—treating health care as a commodity or product that can be purchased only by those who have the money—is untenable for a civilized society. Greenberg argues that the majority of physicians think they have an obligation to treat someone regardless of his or her ability to pay. They reject the view that medical care is primarily a product with an economic value. Greenberg concludes that the United States must join other developed nations in regarding health care as a human right.

AS YOU READ, CONSIDER THE FOLLOWING QUESTIONS:

1. According to Greenberg, what percentage of physicians think that Americans should receive medical care if they need it, regardless of their ability to pay?
2. Which medical organizations does Greenberg say support the notion of health care as a human right?
3. Approximately how many Americans lack health insurance, according to the author?

On the March 4 [2011, *Albuquerque*] *Journal* Op-Ed page, two physicians protested that health care is a commodity, not a right! This refusal to accept the principle that health care is a human right flies in the face of public opinion, physicians' attitudes and the developed world.

Further, the U.S. pattern of health care, in considering health care to be a commodity, has failed to lead the people of our country towards good health, when compared to other nations.

Proponents of universal health care believe health care is a basic human right: A civilized society should guarantee basic health care to its citizens.

Doctors and Medical Organizations Agree

Only a small fraction of U.S. physicians support leaving the health care financing system as it is. Nine in 10 physicians agree that every American should receive needed medical care regardless of ability to pay.

The American College of Physicians, in December 2007, endorsed a system of universal national health insurance to achieve universal health care. The American Academy of Family Physicians advocates a national health system with basic benefits to all individuals. The American Academy of Pediatrics has endorsed the concept that "quality health insurance should be a right, regardless of income, for every child, pregnant woman, their families, and ultimately all individuals." The American College of Obstetrics and Gynecology calls on Congress and the states to "cover all people in the U.S."

FAST FACT

According to the World Health Organization, 100 million people across the globe are pushed below the poverty line as a result of medical bills.

In July 2006, the American College of Surgeons, the American College of Cardiology, and the American Academy of Orthopaedic Surgeons joined other physician organizations in endorsing the "Principles for Reform of the U.S. Health Care System" which states "health care coverage for all is needed to facilitate access to quality health care, which will in turn improve the individual and collective health of society."

Clearly, the majority of U.S. physicians are calling for change, emphasizing the necessity for universal health care.

Health Care Should Not Be a Commodity

The people similarly recognize the mandate for change, transforming health care as a commodity to health care as a human right. Poll after poll, during recent years, has indicated public awareness of the limitations of our health care system and support for a plan that provides universal access to health care.

The U.S. remains as the only country in the developed world that continues to consider health care to be a commodity. All other nations

Americans Think Health Care Is a Human Right

Americans view health care as a right on par with the right to a clean environment, fair pay, and the right to keep personal choices private.

Human Rights
Percent saying health care "strongly should be a human right"

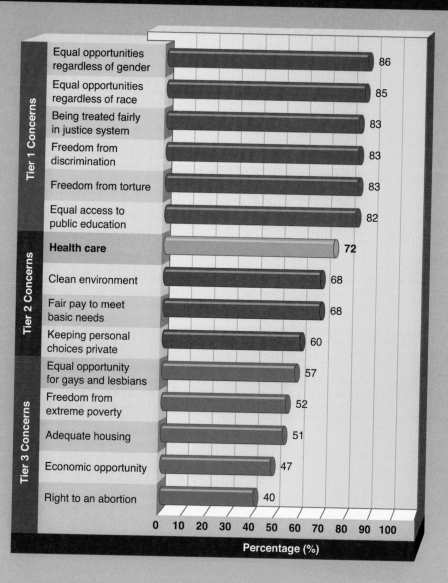

	Percentage (%)
Tier 1 Concerns	
Equal opportunities regardless of gender	86
Equal opportunities regardless of race	85
Being treated fairly in justice system	83
Freedom from discrimination	83
Freedom from torture	83
Equal access to public education	82
Tier 2 Concerns	
Health care	72
Clean environment	68
Fair pay to meet basic needs	68
Keeping personal choices private	60
Tier 3 Concerns	
Equal opportunity for gays and lesbians	57
Freedom from extreme poverty	52
Adequate housing	51
Economic opportunity	47
Right to an abortion	40

Taken from: The Opportunity Agenda. *Human Rights in the US: Opinion Research with Advocates, Journalists, and the General Public*, August 2007.

have implemented a system of health care, often integrating public and private approaches, that mandates that every citizen is supported by a system that provides universal health care.

The U.S. health care system must confront serious questions: Why do we spend so much more on health care, per capita, than other developed countries? Why are our outcomes worse on multiple important measures? Why do we spend up to twice as much per person as countries that provide universal coverage while leaving as many as 50 million Americans without insurance? Why are there such inequities among minority groups in access to health care?

Health care as a human right occupies a firm position in international treaties. The Universal Declaration of Human Rights and the International Covenant on Economic, Social, and Cultural Rights, both passed by the United Nations, recognize the human right to health care.

Humans Have a Right to Health Care

To consider health care as a commodity is to refute the opinions of the populace and those who provide health care, to deny the deficits in our current system, to dispute the world's progress towards improved and universal health care, and to dismiss the principles underlying the human right to health care.

Change of our health care system is beginning. We must all support our finding the best path to universal health care.

EVALUATING THE AUTHOR'S ARGUMENTS:

In this viewpoint Robert Greenberg claims that the health of US citizens lags behind that of many other countries because the United States treats health care as a commodity and not as a right. How might Walter E. Williams, author of the following viewpoint, respond to this claim? Write two to three sentences on how you think Williams might respond. Then state with which author you ultimately agree.

Health Care Is Not a Human Right

Walter E. Williams

> *"For Congress to guarantee a right to health care ... it must diminish someone else's rights, namely their rights to their earnings."*

Health care is not a human right, argues Walter E. Williams in the following viewpoint. He contends that health care is not like free speech, which is endless and unlimited no matter how many people access their right to it; rather, health care is a commodity, and one with a specific price tag. To receive health care costs money; to require the government to pay for it requires using someone else's tax dollars, which Williams likens to stealing. Williams says that if humans have a right to health care, it is only a right to make an appointment with a doctor—they must still manage to pay for the care they receive. Similarly, he says, everyone has the right to travel—but they must buy their own airplane tickets, rental cars, and hotel rooms. Williams concludes that universal health care amounts to stealing from some to give to those who have not earned their share. This is neither moral nor civilized, he maintains.

Williams is a professor of economics at George Mason University.

AS YOU READ, CONSIDER THE FOLLOWING QUESTIONS:
1. What, according to Williams, would come very close to being slavery?
2. What does the author hope most Americans would be offended by?
3. What does the author mean by "noninterference" in the context of the viewpoint?

Most politicians, and probably most Americans, see health care as a right. Thus, whether a person has the means to pay for medical services or not, he is nonetheless entitled to them. Let's ask ourselves a few questions about this vision.

A Form of Slavery

Say a person, let's call him Harry, suffers from diabetes and he has no means to pay a laboratory for blood work, a doctor for treatment and a pharmacy for medication. Does Harry have a right to XYZ lab's and Dr. Jones' services and a prescription from a pharmacist? And, if those services are not provided without charge, should Harry be able to call for criminal sanctions against those persons for violating his rights to health care?

> **FAST FACT**
>
> A study by the Urban Institute in 2008 predicted that extending universal health coverage to uninsured Americans would cost an additional $1.8 trillion from 2010 through 2019.

You say, "Williams, that would come very close to slavery if one person had the right to force someone to serve him without pay." You're right. Suppose instead of Harry being able to force a lab, doctor and pharmacy to provide services without pay, Congress uses its taxing power to take a couple hundred dollars out of the paycheck of some American to give to Harry so that he could pay the lab, doctor and pharmacist. Would there be any difference in principle, namely forcibly using one person to serve the purposes of another? There would be one important strategic difference, that of concealment. Most Americans, I would hope, would be offended by the notion of directly and visibly forcing one person to serve the purposes of another. Congress' use of the tax system to invisibly accomplish the same end is more palatable to the average American.

True Rights Give Without Taking

True rights, such as those in our Constitution, or those considered to be natural or human rights, exist simultaneously among people. That means exercise of a right by one person does not diminish those held by another. In other words, my rights to speech or travel impose no obligations on another except those of noninterference. If we apply ideas behind rights to health care to my rights to speech or travel, my

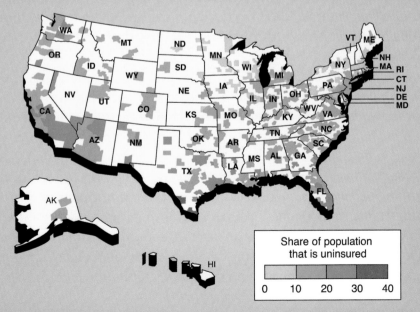

Where Are the Uninsured Americans?

At the end of 2012, about 15 percent of Americans (46 million people) were uninsured. The highest levels of uninsured people were in the West, while the lowest were in the North. There is vast disagreement over whether the government should cover such people, however, or if health care is a human right.

Share of population that is uninsured

0   10   20   30   40

Taken from: Zara Matheson. Martin Prosperity Institute, 2012; and Richard Florida. "Where Are the Most Uninsured Americans?" *Atlantic*, September 26, 2012.

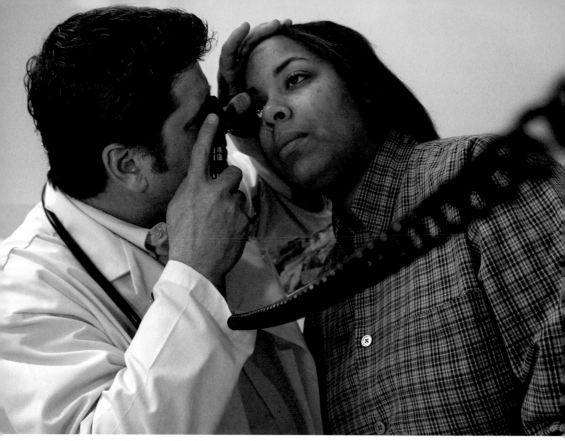

Opponents of universal health care say that requiring the government to pay for health care is the same as stealing from taxpayers.

free speech rights would require government-imposed obligations on others to provide me with an auditorium, television studio or radio station. My right to travel freely would require government-imposed obligations on others to provide me with airfare and hotel accommodations.

For Congress to guarantee a right to health care, or any other good or service, whether a person can afford it or not, it must diminish someone else's rights, namely their rights to their earnings. The reason is that Congress has no resources of its very own. Moreover, there is no Santa Claus, Easter Bunny or Tooth Fairy giving them those resources. The fact that government has no resources of its very own forces one to recognize that in order for government to give one American citizen a dollar, it must first, through intimidation, threats and coercion, confiscate that dollar from some other American. If one person has a right to something he did not earn, of necessity it requires that another person not have a right to something that he did earn.

There Is No Right to Take from Others

To argue that people have a right that imposes obligations on another is an absurd concept. A better term for newfangled rights to health care, decent housing and food is *wishes*. If we called them wishes, I would be in agreement with most other Americans for I, too, wish that everyone had adequate health care, decent housing and nutritious meals. However, if we called them human wishes, instead of human rights, there would be confusion and cognitive dissonance. The average American would cringe at the thought of government punishing one person because he refused to be pressed into making someone else's wish come true.

None of my argument is to argue against charity. Reaching into one's own pockets to assist his fellow man in need is praiseworthy and laudable. Reaching into someone else's pockets to do so is despicable and deserves condemnation.

EVALUATING THE AUTHOR'S ARGUMENTS:

Walter E. Williams is an economics professor. Robert Greenberg, the author of the previous viewpoint, is a physician. In what way does knowing their professions inform your opinion of these authors' arguments? Are you surprised that each one holds the opinion he does? Why or why not?

Chapter 2

What Constitutes a Human Rights Violation?

Palestinian children protest human rights abuses by Israelis in Gaza City in April 2013.

Viewpoint

1

The Death Penalty Is a Human Rights Abuse

Robert Meeropol and Rachel Meeropol

"We view the death penalty as a fundamental human rights abuse."

Government's execution of people violates human rights, argue Robert Meeropol and Rachel Meeropol in the following viewpoint. They contend that no matter what a person has done, that person has an inherent right to live—even if that life is lived out in a jail cell as punishment for a heinous crime. No person, authority, or government has the right to take life from a person, the authors argue. The Meeropols also contend that because the criminal justice system is imperfect, it is possible that an innocent person could be executed. The death penalty is also costly and wasteful and does not deter people from committing terrible crimes, they maintain. The authors also cite the fact that the United Nations' Universal Declaration of Human Rights recognizes that life is a core human right. For all of these reasons they conclude that the death penalty is a human rights abuse and should be abolished.

Robert Meeropol is the director of the Rosenberg Fund for Children. Rachel Meeropol is an attorney at the Center for Constitutional Rights.

AS YOU READ, CONSIDER THE FOLLOWING QUESTIONS:

1. How many death-row inmates have been proven innocent since 1993, according to the authors?
2. How is the death penalty racially and economically skewed, according to the Meeropols?
3. What, according to the authors, would protect the public just as effectively as executions?

Sunday, Oct. 10, is World Day Against the Death Penalty, and on this day, we urge the United States to outlaw this horrible punishment.

As the son and granddaughter of Ethel and Julius Rosenberg, executed by the U.S. government after being convicted of conspiracy to commit espionage at the height of the McCarthy period in 1953, we have a personal reason to abhor the death penalty.

As attorneys, we view the death penalty as a fundamental human rights abuse. And as citizens, we are ashamed that the death penalty is still being carried out in our country.

In 1846, the state of Michigan became one of the earliest governments in the world to abolish the death penalty. More than issues of morality and deterrence, the debate focused on a fundamental question: Does a government have the right to put people to death?

FAST FACT

In September 2009 authorities tried to execute Romell Broom for the 1984 abduction, rape, and killing of a fourteen-year-old girl. The attempt to put him to death via lethal injection took more than two hours because authorities could not find a suitable vein. During the lengthy process, Broom developed anxiety, cried, and suffered multiple needle pricks. His lawyers and opponents of the death penalty called his botched execution "torture."

There are many compelling reasons to answer no.

First of all, the death penalty diminishes the humanity of everyone it touches. As Sojourner Truth told the Michigan legislature during one debate on whether to reinstate capital punishment, "We are the makers of murderers if we do it."

Second, since our system of justice can never be mistake-free, it is inevitable that an error will be made in a capital case and an innocent person will be executed. In fact, DNA evidence has demonstrated the innocence of at least 17 death-row inmates since 1993, according to the Innocence Project.

Third, the question of cost is also compelling. At a time when states face massive budget shortfalls, a study examining the cost of the death penalty in Kansas found that death penalty cases are 70 percent more

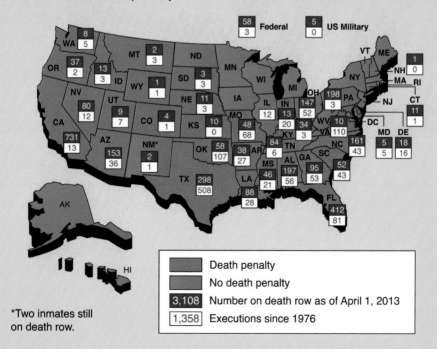

Death Penalty in America

As of 2013, seventeen states (plus the District of Columbia) had abolished the death penalty.

Legend:
- Death penalty
- No death penalty
- 3,108 Number on death row as of April 1, 2013
- 1,358 Executions since 1976

*Two inmates still on death row.

Taken from: Death Penalty Information Centre; NAACP Legal Defense and Educational Fund.

Opponents of the death penalty argue that every human being has the right to live.

expensive than comparable non-death penalty cases. A report by the Urban Institute found that taxpayers paid at least $37.2 million for each of five executions carried out in Maryland.

Fourth, the death penalty disproportionately falls on poor people and people of color. Blacks and Latinos make up more than 55 percent of the current death row population, despite comprising only about 25 percent of the U.S. population. The vast majority of people on death row are poor.

Fifth, the death penalty is not an effective deterrent. States that use it don't have lower murder rates than states that do not. Plus, life imprisonment would protect the public just as well as execution does.

Finally, there is a more fundamental reason. In the aftermath of World War II, the United States took a leadership role in drafting an "international bill of rights" that recognized all people have certain inherent rights. This core human rights document, the Universal Declaration of Human Rights, put it simply: Life is a human right. This makes the death penalty our deepest human rights abuse. As long as governments have the right to extinguish our lives, they maintain the power to deny us access to every other right.

A human rights perspective on capital punishment has the additional advantage of being permanent. If capital punishment could somehow be fixed—the cost cut, the racial and class biases removed, all possibilities for error eliminated—the government still can't execute, because it violates human rights.

On this eighth World Day Against the Death Penalty, let us reaffirm our commitment to human rights and reassert our common humanity by demanding that our government stop killing our fellow human beings.

EVALUATING THE AUTHOR'S ARGUMENTS:

To make their argument that the death penalty violates human rights, the Meeropols argue that every human being has the right to live. Do you agree that this right should apply to criminals who have killed other people? When a person commits murder, do they forfeit their human rights? Explain your reasoning.

The Death Penalty Does Not Violate Human Rights

Charles Lane

"The death penalty . . . should remain available for the 'worst of the worst' offenders."

In the following viewpoint Charles Lane argues that the death penalty does not violate human rights. He considers the case of Anders Breivik, a Norwegian man who in 2011 shot to death sixty-nine young people at a summer camp, as well as killing several others in a bombing. Lane says Breivik is utterly unrepentant for these murders, and in robbing these people of their lives, he lost his right to keep his own. Execution is the only just punishment for someone who commits such an unthinkable, inhumane act. Norway does not have the death penalty, so Breivik will receive a much lighter sentence—which Lane finds reprehensible. If life is to be worth anything, it must matter when people kill others, he maintains. He concludes that brutal killers deserve death, paying for their crimes with their own lives.

Lane is a columnist for the *Washington Post*.

AS YOU READ, CONSIDER THE FOLLOWING QUESTIONS:
1. What is the maximum penalty that Lane says Anders Breivik can receive for his crimes?
2. What percentage of people in Connecticut does Lane say support the death penalty?
3. Who is Thomas Indrebo, as mentioned by the author?

If anyone personifies evil, it is Anders Breivik. The 33-year-old Norwegian violently disrupted his country's usual peace on July 22, 2011, by gunning down 69 mostly young people at a summer camp. A bomb he planted in Oslo killed eight others. He did it all to defend Norway against multiculturalism, he later raved.

Killers Deserve Death

Yet, on one point, Breivik is not talking crazy. At his trial, which began April 16, [2012,] he pronounced the maximum penalty for his actions—21 years in prison, or longer if the government meets certain conditions—"pathetic." He "would have respected" the death penalty, Breivik said. Of course, he won't get it; Norway abolished capital punishment long ago.

Norway has suffered deeply because of Breivik, and I don't mean to add insult to injury. But this situation illustrates what's wrong with banning the death penalty in all cases. If executing an innocent man is the worst-case scenario for proponents of the death penalty, then threatening Breivik with prison is the reductio ad absurdum [showing that a proposition leads to an absurd conclusion] of death-penalty abolitionism.

Anti-death-penalty sentiment is hardly limited to Europe. Last week [in April 2012] Connecticut Gov. Dan Malloy signed a bill abolishing capital punishment, which means that no future Anders Breivik need fear execution in that state. Sixteen other states have no death penalty; California voters will get a chance to join them in a November referendum. [California voters elected to keep the state's death penalty.]

In the United States, abolitionist arguments are gaining traction, especially claims about the high cost of lengthy death-penalty litigation and the risk of executing people by mistake. Malloy also cited a "moral component" to his decision.

The Worst of the Worst

Such practical and moral concerns are at their most understandable in run-of-the-mill convenience-store murder cases, where the risk of error seems relatively high compared with the benefits of punishing murder with death.

But Breivik's was no ordinary crime. It presents the special case of a cold-blooded massacre of children by a political terrorist whose guilt is unquestionable and who remains utterly unrepentant; indeed, he told the court that he would kill again if given the opportunity.

What is morally worse: putting the author of this bloodbath to death or letting him live, with the accompanying risk—however small—that he might broadcast his message to receptive audiences from jail, or escape, or one day litigate his way to freedom?

There is no scientific answer. To oppose the death penalty regardless of the crime or the consequences of letting the perpetrator live is

Self-confessed mass murderer Anders Breivik gives a fascist-style salute after being sentenced for the killing of more than seventy people in Norway in 2011. Many believe that Breivik's acts deny him his right to life.

a consistent and principled position. If Norwegians consider doing so a point of pride, that's their choice.

Justice Is Truly Moral

In Connecticut, 62 percent of registered voters support the death penalty for murder, according to a Quinnipiac University poll published last month [March 2012]—so it took some political courage for the legislature and governor to do what they did.

But note that the Connecticut law is not retroactive: It does not apply to the 11 men already on death row, including two sentenced to death for a 2007 home invasion in which they raped and strangled a mother, murdered her two daughters and then set the bodies ablaze.

It seems a tad inconsistent, and somewhat less than courageous, to condemn the injustice and immorality of the death penalty while allowing it in 11 more cases.

> ## FAST FACT
>
> In 1976 the US Supreme Court in *Gregg v. Georgia* affirmed that the death penalty does not violate the Eighth Amendment, which forbids cruel and unusual punishment, nor the Fourteenth Amendment, which prohibits depriving a person of life without due process of law.

This tells me that the Connecticut politicians who voted to ban future capital punishment still find it hard to argue against the death penalty in every specific case, no matter how ghastly.

Humans Have a Right to Retribution

The stubborn fact is that death-penalty abolitionism runs counter to one of humanity's oldest and most persistent moral intuitions: that there should be condign retribution for the most monstrous transgressions.

Even in Norway, Breivik's rampage caused some second thoughts. Immediately after his crimes last summer, a man named Thomas Indrebo observed online that "the death penalty is the only just sentence in this case!!!!!!" Indrebo was later assigned as

Americans Consistently Favor the Death Penalty

Year after year the majority of Americans support use of the death penalty, in part because they believe convicted murderers sacrifice their right to life.

"Are you in favor of the death penalty for a person convicted of murder?"

Date	Favor	Oppose	Unsure
October 2011	61	35	4
October 2010	64	29	6
October 2009	65	31	5
October 2008	64	30	5
October 2007	69	27	4
May 2006	65	28	7
October 2005	64	30	6
October 2004	65	31	5
May 2004	71	26	3
October 2003	64	32	4
May 2003	74	24	2
October 2002	70	25	5
May 2002	72	25	3
October 2001	68	26	6
May 2001	65	27	8
February 2001	67	25	8
September 2000	67	28	5
February 1999	71	22	7
May 1995	77	13	10
September 1994	80	16	4
June 1991	76	18	6

Taken from: Gallup Poll, October 6–9, 2011.

a lay judge in Breivik's trial and had to be dismissed because of his comment.

That was the right call, legally. But I wonder if the Breivik case will cause more people in Europe to ask whether there really is no place in civilization for capital punishment.

Both abroad and at home, we need less polarized debate, less moralizing—and more honest legislative efforts to reconcile valid concerns about the death penalty with the public's clear and consistent belief that it should remain available for the "worst of the worst" offenders.

EVALUATING THE AUTHOR'S ARGUMENTS:

In the previous viewpoint Robert Meeropol and Rachel Meeropol argue that life is a fundamental human right that is violated by the death penalty. In this viewpoint Charles Lane argues that some murderers deserve to die and that society has a right to seek retribution for heinous crimes. With which viewpoint do you agree? Does the death penalty violate or uphold human rights? Explain your reasoning and cite evidence from the text that swayed you.

Drone Warfare Violates Human Rights

Ramesh Thakur

"Extrajudicial killings using . . . drones pose a challenge to international law and may constitute war crimes."

In the following viewpoint Ramesh Thakur argues that drone warfare violates human rights. Drones are unmanned combat weapons that are operated by remote control. They are increasingly used by the US military because they protect soldiers from having to engage in ground combat. But Thakur contends that because they are machines, drones kill indiscriminately— they cannot tell adults from children or enemies from innocents. As a result, drone warfare has killed many innocent men, women, and children, he points out. Furthermore, Thakur argues that drones facilitate assassinations that circumvent compliance with international humanitarian law that aim to help make sure that targets are accurate and warranted. People are being murdered just because they have the misfortune of living in certain parts of the world, Thakur maintains. He concludes that this is a violation of their human rights and a violation of international humanitarian law.

Thakur is a professor in the Crawford School of Public Policy at Australian National University and director of the school's Centre for Nuclear Non-Proliferation and Disarmament.

AS YOU READ, CONSIDER THE FOLLOWING QUESTIONS:
1. Who is Tariq Khan, as mentioned by the author?
2. How many people does Thakur say have been killed by drone strikes in the last eight years?
3. Who does the author say qualifies as a combatant in a drone strike zone?

As in other aspects of human life, the march of military technology has greatly outpaced the laws and institutions to regulate the behavior they make possible. The [Barack] Obama administration has so greatly expanded the [George W.] Bush policy of drone strikes as to leave neutral observers queasy about the legal regime governing the new tools of warfare.

Killers That Strike from the Sky

Last October [2011], Pakistani tribal elders from North Waziristan traveled to Islamabad to protest against the U.S. drone strikes. With them was a 16-year old boy named Tariq Khan. He did not want to return home for fear of the drones. He did and died in a drone attack four days after the Islamabad *jirga* (tribal assembly).

In September 2011, Anwar al-Awlaki, an American of Yemeni descent, was killed by a U.S. drone strike somewhere in Yemen. His 16-year old son (that is, a juvenile) was killed in a followup strike some weeks later.

These terrifying unseen killers that strike silently from the sky are a potent, unnerving symbol of unchecked and potentially cruel and capricious American power. Independent estimates suggest that between 2,000 and 3,000 people have been killed in such U.S. strikes in the last eight years, around 80 percent during the Obama administration. Washington columnist Aaron David Miller concluded that "as shown through his stepped-up drone campaign, Barack Obama has become George W. Bush on steroids."

Killing Without Knowing Who the Enemy Is

Three-quarters are claimed to be militants. Others claim that drone strikes kill seven times as many followers as top-level terrorists. An Alice in Wonderland definition eases legal and moral concerns. The administration counts all military-age males in a drone strike zone as combatants unless they are clearly proven—posthumously—to have been innocent. This is certainly convenient in claiming minimum loss of innocent civilian lives.

Given the memorable record of the U.S. intelligence on the "slam dunk" evidence proving Iraq President Saddam Hussein's weapons of mass destruction, the secretive determinations of guilt and imposition of capital punishment by intelligence-bureaucratic processes instead of open and contested judicial trials is troubling.

Having criticized the Bush administration for the secret practices of surveillance, interrogation and detention, Obama has dramatically expanded the practice of secretly putting people on kill lists. Drone warfare greatly stretches the boundaries of the imperial presidency relative to Congressional checks and judicial oversight.

> **FAST FACT**
>
> The Bureau of Investigative Journalism in the United Kingdom estimates that since 2004, the United States has launched 362 drone attacks that have killed anywhere from 2,629 to 3,461 people in Pakistan. As many as 891 were civilians and 176 were children.

Not Consistent with International Law

It also raises the question: Is the extrajudicial killing of foreigners (and Americans living abroad) following a bureaucratic determination, as Obama is doing, more or less frightening and morally reprehensible than capturing them and sending them to detention and torture in Guantanamo Bay, as Bush did and Obama condemned?

The policy is justified on grounds of neutralizing imminent threats. In a speech on March 5, Attorney General Eric Holder explained that "an 'imminent threat' incorporates considerations of the relevant window of opportunity to act, the possible harm that missing the

Drones Kill Innocent People

In 2012 the Human Rights Clinic at Columbia Law School and the Center for Civilians in Conflict reported that other individuals are often swept up in drone strikes. Civilians and "persons of unknown status" make up thousands of those killed in drone warfare.

Estimated Number of People Killed by US Drone Strikes in Pakistan, According to the Following Organizations

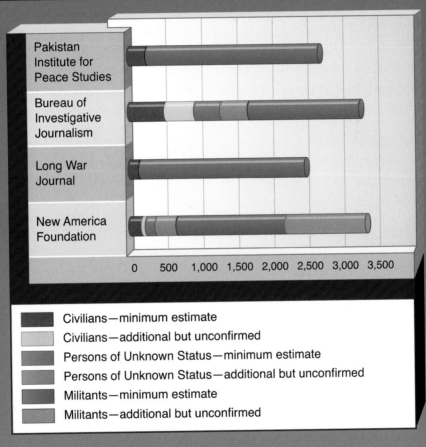

Civilians—minimum estimate
Civilians—additional but unconfirmed
Persons of Unknown Status—minimum estimate
Persons of Unknown Status—additional but unconfirmed
Militants—minimum estimate
Militants—additional but unconfirmed

Taken from: Adam Serwer. "The Drone Unknowns." *Mother Jones*, October 1, 2012.

window would cause to civilians, and the likelihood of heading off future disastrous attacks against the United States."

Because of al-Qaida's proven ability and willingness to attack with little or no notice and cause devastating casualties, he added, the president is not required "to delay action until some theoretical end-stage of planning—when the precise time, place, and manner of an attack become clear. Such a requirement would create an unacceptably high risk that our efforts would fail, and that Americans would be killed."

This is not a definition of "imminent" that most scholars of international law would recognize. Holder did not address some fundamental questions: How is a threat determined, what counts as decisive evidence on determining the status of operational commander, and how do officials conclude that arrest is not feasible?

Remote-Controlled War Is an Affront to Humanity

The growing drone dependency owes to its convenience: It is faster, less complicated and more expedient to eliminate the enemy terrorist than to arrest and try him. It also eliminates the risk to U.S. soldiers.

Pakistanis stand inside their home after it was destroyed by a missile fired from a US drone. In many cases US drone strikes have caused the deaths of innocent people.

But convenience is not enough to justify remote-controlled war in law and international humanitarian law (IHL). U.N. Special Rapporteur Philip Alston argues that extrajudicial killings using weapons like drones pose a challenge to international law and may constitute war crimes as intelligence agencies "do not generally operate within a framework that places appropriate emphasis upon ensuring compliance" with IHL.

Moreover, "because operators are based thousands of miles away from the battlefield, and undertake operations entirely through computer screens and remote audio-feed," they risk developing "a 'Playstation mentality' to killing." In the aftermath of the terrorist attacks of Sept. 11, 2001, adherence to human rights law, the laws of war and IHL had softened. "The result has been the displacement of clear legal standards with a vaguely defined license to kill, and the creation of a major accountability vacuum."

Drones Kill Everybody

In sum, there is both a legal and a strategic problem with the increasing use of drones to kill the enemy:

- Justice dispensed by drones cannot be reconciled with the rule of law.
- Sir Sherard Cowper-Coles, Britain's former special representative to Afghanistan and Pakistan, insists that drone attacks are counterproductive because of the hatred they generate.

In a now-famous memo on the war on terror (Oct. 16, 2003), U.S. Defense Secretary Donald Rumsfeld posed the prophetic and critical question: "Are we capturing, killing or deterring and dissuading more terrorists every day than the madrassas and the radical clerics are recruiting, training and deploying against us?"

What he did not ask was the cause-and-effect link between U.S. successes in capturing, torturing and killing terrorist suspects, and more terrorists being recruited in consequence. It was in this sense that Sir Ivor Roberts, the British ambassador to Italy, remarked to the annual meeting of British and Italian political leaders in Rome on Sept. 19, 2004, that al-Qaida had cause to celebrate the re-election of President George W. Bush. For "Bush is al-Qaida's best recruiting sergeant."

Thus it was that Pakistani Faisal Shahzad, the failed Times Square bomber of May 2010, when asked about potential innocent victims of his plot, replied: "U.S. drone strikes don't see children, they don't see anybody. They kill women, children; they kill everybody."

EVALUATING THE AUTHOR'S ARGUMENTS:

In this viewpoint Ramesh Thakur describes drones as inhumane weapons. In the following viewpoint Steven A. Emerson describes drones as humane weapons. List at least two arguments made by each author for why a drone is a humane or inhumane weapon, state which position you think is stronger, and then explain why.

In Defense of Drones

Steven A. Emerson

"[Drones] have a much smaller range of collateral damage than the . . . bombs used in earlier wars [and] . . . can be guided with far greater precision."

Drone warfare does not violate human rights, argues Steven A. Emerson in the following viewpoint. In fact, Emerson argues that the opposite is true: Drones have made war more precise and less deadly for both soldiers and noncombatants in enemy areas. He explains that drones are much more sophisticated than weapons used in past wars—they can strike an area more precisely, greatly reducing the range of collateral damage. This means fewer damaged buildings and a smaller range of explosions, which Emerson contends means fewer innocent people hurt and killed. The military must also follow a rigorous process for executing a drone strike, the author maintains, which ensures the targeted kill is carried out with intent and proper clearance. Emerson says people who oppose drone strikes want the United States to fight a brutal enemy with one hand tied behind its back. He concludes that drones make war more effective, efficient, and humane.

The Pentagon follows a six-step process that can go as high as the president of the United States before launching an aerial strike against a suspected terrorist target, according to military documents filed in federal court this week.

If commanders or intelligence officers in the field want to use an unmanned drone to fire a missile or have a bomber drop a laser-guided bomb on a suspected terrorist, says a briefing document prepared by the Pentagon's joint staff last November, they have to follow these steps:

- Identify the target.
- Determine if the target is a fully developed threat.
- Evaluate whether the intelligence supports the targeting.
- Consider whether eliminating the target would further US interests.
- Weigh domestic and international laws to determine what rules apply.
- Strike the target and analyze the results.

According to the Pentagon document, titled "Joint Targeting Cycle and Collateral Damage Estimation Methodology," while an aerial attack during the Vietnam war would cause collateral damage up to 400 feet from its intended target, that range has been cut to 40 feet. That's because of improved bombs and missiles that carry smaller payloads and have more sophisticated guidance systems.

For example, the Predator and Reaper unmanned drones, which are most frequently used in these attacks, use Hellfire missiles, which have a much smaller range of collateral damage than the 500 lbs. "dumb" bombs used in earlier wars. These drones also use laser-guided explosives that can be guided with far greater precision than even those to great fanfare in the first Gulf war almost 20 years ago.

The unusual release of such information is because of the ACLU's ongoing challenge to the Obama administration's drone program.

On Aug. 30, the ACLU filed suit on behalf of Nasser al-Awlaki, father of Anwar al-Awlaki, an American citizen who now leads al Qaeda on the Arabian Peninsula and has been a popular propagandist for the movement. The case says Obama and military officials have been given "sweeping authority to impose death sentences" without legal approval.

But the Pentagon's defense shows how careful the government is with such attacks.

Advocates of drone warfare argue that since drones are much more precise in hitting their targets, fewer innocent people are killed by them than are unintentionally killed by conventional weapons.

Besides the six-step process, there are a number of "no strike" zones and targets, including religious centers, medical facilities, schools and public utilities. Attacking any of these requires direct approval from the president or the secretary of defense.

The increased use of drones has been an integral part of the Obama administration's counterterrorism policy. Earlier this year, CIA Director Leon Panetta reported that "those operations are seriously disrupting al Qaeda . . . It's pretty clear from all the intelligence we are getting that they are having a very difficult time putting together any kind of command and control, that they are scrambling and that we really do have them on the run."

Awlaki's complicity in terrorist attacks is unquestioned. Since late 2009, Awlaki "has taken on an increasingly operational role in [al Qaeda]," said Director of National Intelligence James Clapper in a statement filed in the court case in August. Awlaki, Clapper said, has recruited terrorists and planned and facilitated attacks in the United States and abroad. He is also a contributing editor for the terrorist organization's cyber magazine, *Inspire*, in which the group calls for the targeting of civilian centers throughout the United States. In one such call to jihad, the magazine says: "The ideal location is a place where there are a maximum number of pedestrian and the least number of vehicles. In fact if you can get through to 'pedestrian only' locations that exist in some downtown (city center) areas, that would be fabulous."

> ## FAST FACT
>
> A 2012 poll conducted by ABC News and the *Washington Post* revealed that 83 percent of Americans approve of the US government's use of drones to target terrorist suspects overseas.

Contrast this with the Pentagon document, whose unnamed author concludes that "never before has a nation taken such measures and resources to reduce the likelihood of civilian casualties."

Based on Clapper's testimony and Awlaki's own actions, the former imam at mosques in San Diego, Denver and Washington fits the criteria spelled out in the targeting document. He's called for the killing of US troops and civilians and inspired Maj. Nidal Hasan, the

Drone Strikes Are Very Accurate

According to the New American Foundation, which has analyzed drone strike data, drones become more accurate each year. During their initial years of use, civilians made up as much as 61 percent of the dead in an attack. By 2012, however, civilians were just 2 percent of those killed. Supporters argue this is a very low rate of civilian death for warfare.

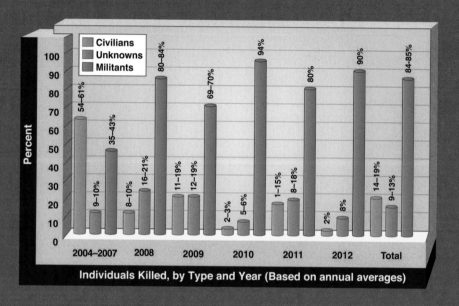

Taken from: "The Year of the Drone." New America Foundation, 2012. http://counterterrorism.newamerica.net/drones.

Army officer accused of killing 13 people at Fort Hood last November. Clearly, if a goal is eliminating a key leader in al Qaeda, then eliminating Awlaki with an airstrike is no different than the continued attempts to kill the Taliban's Mullah Omar the same way.

The ACLU may consider targeted killings immoral, but is it more immoral than the widespread use of human shields by the Taliban? Than the targeting by al Qaeda of commercial airliners? Awlaki would deny everyone else the rights the ACLU claims he has. Meanwhile, 17 international troops were killed in the last month trying to protect the freedom of Afghanis.

If the ACLU is filing lawsuits on behalf of protecting US-born terrorists from targeted assassinations, why isn't the ACLU filing lawsuits on behalf of American soldiers who have become corollary assassination targets while being handcuffed in fighting those who killed 3,000 Americans?

EVALUATING THE AUTHOR'S ARGUMENTS:

Both Ramesh Thakur (author of the previous viewpoint) and Steven A. Emerson in the present viewpoint discuss the case of Anwar al-Awlaki, who was killed in a drone strike in 2011. But Emerson points to Awlaki's killing as an example of a humane and accurate drone attack, while Thakur questions the legality of whether an American citizen should be assassinated by machine rather than being brought home to stand trial for his crimes. Do some outside research on the case of Awlaki. Do you think he is an example in favor of or against drone strikes? Explain your reasoning and be sure to cite the sources that influenced you.

Sweatshops Violate Human Rights

Bama Athreya

"Severe cases of violations of workers rights have been reported [in sweatshops]."

Bama Athreya is part of the International Labor Rights Forum, a group that works toward eliminating sweatshops and creating just and humane working conditions worldwide. In the following viewpoint taken from her testimony before a District of Columbia government committee, Athreya argues that sweatshops violate human rights. She has personally visited such factories and describes terrible conditions in which young people work for long hours and little pay; by the time they pay for their cramped, uncomfortable living quarters and utilities, they have almost no money left over. Athreya contends that these conditions amount to a type of indentured servitude and that it is immoral to make profits on the backs of these near-slaves. Athreya maintains that the garment industry must be more tightly regulated so that companies buy clothes only from factories that treat their workers humanely and justly.

AS YOU READ, CONSIDER THE FOLLOWING QUESTIONS:
1. How many girls worked in the Indonesian factory discussed by the author?
2. Recount the living conditions at the factory described by Athreya.
3. What is the Hui Yang Charming Garment factory, as mentioned by the author?

Thank you for the opportunity to testify today about the problem of sweatshops, and the solution to this problem provided by our proposed Sweatfree DC [District of Columbia] amendment to the Omnibus Procurement Reform Amendment Act of 2010 introduced by Council member Mary Cheh. I represent the International Labor Rights Forum, or ILRF, an advocacy organization dedicated to achieving just and humane treatment of workers worldwide. One of ILRF's campaigns is SweatFree Communities, which works to improve working conditions in apparel and other labor-intensive global industries by promoting the adoption and enforcement of sweatfree policy at all levels of US government. The campaign's efforts have resulted, to date, in the adoption of sweatfree procurement policies by over 180 public entities in the US, including the states of California, Illinois, New York, Maine, New Jersey and Pennsylvania.

Stories of Sweat and Hardship

Let me start by explaining the problem that our amendment and the subsequent Sweatfree Procurement Policy that it would create, has the potential to address. Over the past three decades, we have witnessed the wide scale flight of domestic production of apparel to low-wage countries with unsafe and exploitative working conditions. We are not an organization that opposes global trade, per se, but we cannot ignore the fact that the flight of these industries is driven by the 'race to the bottom.' Multinational corporations seek out production destinations where there is little or no regulation of labor or environmental conditions; they find such destinations in the developing world.

I lived and worked with young women in Cambodia and Indonesia where I have also had the opportunity to meet and have frank conversations with young women producing garments for the US market. Mari was a young friend of mine in Indonesia, working in a garment factory. Her factory was a small warehouse, where about 300 girls worked, all sewing T-shirts for export to the US and Europe. When it rained the girls would stand at their machines, ankle-deep in water, as there was not sufficient drainage. The girls typically worked 10 to 12 hours per day, six days a week and a half-day on Sundays.

Many labor activists consider this garment factory in Indonesia, as well as many such Indonesian factories, to be sweatshops that violate the workers' human rights.

They were not paid for overtime, and were forced to meet targets of production to receive their wages. Wages were often paid late, as the factory manager claimed he had not been paid by the buyer. The girls lived in small shacks in the area nearby the factory; they shared rooms, often six to eight people to a rented room. By the time the girls had paid for rent, food, and water (yes, they did not have access to potable water), they had virtually no money left over for any other purpose. Mari and her friends, and their working conditions, were so much like the conditions I saw in many other countries. This is the way an unregulated apparel industry treats its workers.

Sweatshop Workers Make American Products

Do these things happen in factories producing uniforms and other goods for the US market? We can assure you they do. To cite just a few examples: Collectively, from 2004–2009 DC has purchased over $9 million in apparel from Morgan's, or Jimmie Muscatello's, and currently it holds the single largest apparel contract with the city for over $2 million. Morgan's supplies numerous brands including Blauer. Blauer sourced some of its apparel from the Hui Yang Charming Garments factory in China where severe cases of violations of workers rights have been reported. Because DC does not require Morgan's to provide up-to-date factory disclosure information so that third party investigations can be carried out, it is impossible to know what connection DC has to this factory.

> # FAST FACT
>
> According to the US Bureau of Democracy, Human Rights, and Labor, in 2011 the minimum wage for clothing factory workers in Guatemala was $7.61 per day—less than half the income needed ($570 a month) for a family's basic needs.

Ways to End Worker Abuse

We urge the committee to promote a new legislative remedy for workers' rights abuses in the global supply chains that sell products to the District of Columbia by supporting the addition of our proposed Sweatfree DC amendment to Bill 18-610. This is not only good for workers, but good for the district and good for business. By ensur-

© Fair-Trade Cartoons.

ing that tax dollars do not subsidize profiteering from human rights abuses, a Sweatfree Procurement Policy will help create a more stable and sustainable business environment. By establishing a sweatfree manufacturing code of conduct and requiring vendors to disclose factory locations and wages, the bill will create an even playing field for all bidders. No one will be able to undercut anyone else with sweatshop products.

The District of Columbia can also use this as an opportunity to demonstrate its leadership by joining with Maine, Pennsylvania and other state and municipal governments through the Sweatfree Purchasing Consortium. States and cities have taken this step as they face the challenge of finding resources for, and expertise in, factory monitoring and remediation programs. By pooling resources and expertise, public institutions will be able to ensure that all vendors have access to reliable and up-to-date information about sweatfree suppliers. A professional and independent human rights monitor will provide this information to all consortium members. Collaboration with other public entities will also foster common standards across the nation, helping businesses to expand by using a single set of information to comfortably bid on jobs to any and all consortium members.

EVALUATING THE AUTHOR'S ARGUMENTS:

Bama Athreya describes long hours, little pay, and uncomfortable, even dangerous working conditions that would be unheard of in the United States. She claims that overseas workers should not be subjected to these conditions. How would Jacob G. Hornberger, author of the following viewpoint, respond to this claim? Write two to three sentences on what Hornberger might say; then state with which author you agree and why.

Viewpoint 6

Sweatshops Do Not Violate Human Rights

Jacob G. Hornberger

In the following viewpoint Jacob G. Hornberger argues that sweatshops do not violate human rights. He agrees that working conditions in sweatshops are less than ideal, but this is compared with American standards of working conditions, he contends; in reality, sweatshops are the best places to work in the countries in which they exist. If sweatshops closed down, workers would be condemned to even poorer jobs—or worse, they would have no job at all and be doomed to abject poverty, starvation, and death. Enforcing regulations and laws just makes things worse, maintains Hornberger, because the only way to raise standards of living and working conditions is to allow unfettered economic growth. He concludes that people who oppose sweatshops are well-meaning but misguided and actually end up hurting the poor more than helping them.

Hornberger is founder and president of the libertarian public policy institute the Future of Freedom Foundation.

"Sweatshops help the poor."

AS YOU READ, CONSIDER THE FOLLOWING QUESTIONS:
  1. What job does Hornberger say would be worse than working in a sweatshop?
  2. Why, according to Hornberger, did whole families work in sweatshops during the Industrial Revolution?
  3. What will make standards of living soar, according to the author?

"I love sweatshops."

That was how economics professor Benjamin Powell, our Economic Liberty Lecture Series speaker last night [April 23, 2012], wrapped up his excellent talk on the benefits of sweatshops. An overflow crowd, mostly composed of George Mason University students, was treated to an eloquent exposition of why and how sweatshops help the poor.

This is one of the things that liberals, who are generally steadfast opponents of sweatshops, just don't get. Their hearts are in the right place. They're concerned about the plight of those at the bottom of the economic ladder (although their support of immigration controls belies that concern).

But as I have repeatedly pointed out, when it comes to economics, liberals just have a blind spot. They do not understand that the policies that they advocate to help the poor actually do the opposite—they hurt the poor. One of the best examples of this phenomenon relates to sweatshops.

An Inappropriate Comparison

As Powell pointed out, liberals point to the horrific working conditions that exist in sweatshops. And they're right—such conditions are horrific, especially when compared with standard working conditions here in the United States.

But that's not the correct comparison. The correct comparison is between the working conditions in the sweatshop and the working conditions in alternative lines of available work.

In other words, what if a Third World sweatshop was closed down? What then would the worker do to sustain his life? Powell pointed out that the worker would end up in a lower-paying job with even worse working conditions than existed in the sweatshop. Doing back-breaking manual labor on a farm at lower pay is just one example Powell pointed to.

Sweatshops Are the Best Option

So, when people choose to go work in a sweatshop, they're making a rational choice—they are choosing the best of all the alternatives. When liberals succeed in closing down a sweatshop, they're condemning the workers to an even worse plight, perhaps even starvation.

Consider, for example, the sweatshops in the United States in the 1800s and early 1900s. Men were sending their wives and children into sweatshops, where they would have to work long hours for low pay under horrible, oftentimes dangerous, conditions.

Liberals suggest that those men hated their wives and their children, as manifested by their sending them to work in sweatshops, and that it was only interventionist laws that saved mothers and children from such enmity.

Whereas many Americans consider this and other foreign factories to be inhumane sweatshops, others argue that such places at least provide an income to people who would otherwise have no resources at all.

Sweatshop Workers Fare Better than Other Workers in Their Country

A 2012 study reported in the *American Journal of Economics & Sociology* investigated minimum wages for a variety of industries in El Salvador. It found that compared to other industries, clothing and manufacturing factory work (performed in sweatshops) has the third-highest minimum wage and a wage that far exceeds all agricultural and farming jobs. The authors concluded that workers in these positions make more than workers in other industries, and thus have better opportunities relative to those in their country.

Salvadoran Daily Minimum Wage by Industry

Industry	Wage
Business and Service Industry	$6.41
Industry (not clothing and manufacturing)	$6.27
Clothing and Manufacturing Factories	**$5.57**
Seasonal Agriculture/Coffee	$4.34
Harvesting Coffee	$3.28
Seasonal Agriculture/Sugar Mills	$3.16
Agriculture and Livestock Industry	$3.00
Harvesting Sugar Cane	$2.78
Harvesting Cotton	$2.50

Taken from: David Skarbek, Emily Skarbek, Brian Skarbek, and Erin Skarbek. "Sweatshops, Opportunity Costs, and Non-Monetary Compensation: Evidence from El Salvador." *American Journal of Economics & Sociology*, vol. 71, no. 3, July 2012, pp. 539–561.

Nonsense. The reason that men were sending their wives and children into sweatshops was not because they hated them but because this was the only way to enable everyone in the family to survive. If the alternative to working in a sweatshop is death by starvation, what husband and father is going to say to his wife and children, "I just don't want you working in bad conditions and so I'm going to make you stay home and starve to death"?

Thus, for the Industrial Revolution the proper comparison is not between working conditions in the sweatshops and working conditions today. The proper comparison is between working conditions in the sweatshops and working conditions before the Industrial Revolution. Life preceding the Industrial Revolution was [as seventeenth-century philosopher Thomas Hobbes put it,] "nasty, brutish, and short" for most people, especially the poor. The Industrial Revolution, as bad as it was, at least provided a means by which people could survive.

Economic Freedom Makes the Difference

How come some nations are wealthier than others? That's what liberals never ask. They just see a massive amount of wealth in certain societies and assume that it's a given. Then, they spend their time figuring out ways to confiscate the wealth and give it to the poor, which over time dooms the entire society, especially the poor, to lower standards of living.

Or liberals go into Third World nations and advocate interventionist laws to try to duplicate working conditions that exist in wealthier countries. In other words, they think that the government, just by passing laws that regulate economic activity, can bring into existence a wealthy country.

Nonsense again. As Powell pointed out, the key to economic development and rising standards of living, especially for the poor, lies in economic liberty, free enterprise, and the rising level of productive capital. As people, including the rich, save more money, that money goes into tools and equipment, which makes workers more productive, which means higher real wage rates.

> **FAST FACT**
>
> A 2004 working paper by the Independent Institute asserts that in ten countries where sweatshops operate, apparel workers are paid more than the national average income. They receive three to seven times more than the average pay in the Dominican Republic, Haiti, Honduras, and Nicaragua.

Thus, what took women and children out of the U.S. sweatshops was not interventionist laws but rather rising levels of savings, capital, and wage rates.

Get Government Out of Labor

So, therein lies the key to raising the standard of living of the poor around the world. To put it simply: To help the poor, stop government from helping the poor. End all governmental wars on poverty. Prevent government from regulating or controlling economic activity. Abolish income taxes and tariffs. Leave people free to engage in economic enterprise free of government control or direction. Leave people free to accumulate unlimited amounts of wealth. Leave charity entirely to the private decisions of individuals.

Within a relatively short period of time, standards of living will begin to soar, and the biggest beneficiaries will be the poor.

Finally, Powell brought up an interesting point regarding immigration. What better way to improve the standard of living of people working in horrific conditions in Third World sweatshops than to leave them free to immigrate to the United States, where they stand to earn much higher income in better working conditions?

Alas, however, it is only us libertarians who call for open borders. For liberals, who profess to love the poor, and conservatives, who profess to love the rich, open immigration is anathema.

EVALUATING THE AUTHOR'S ARGUMENTS:

Jacob G. Hornberger paints the decision to work in a sweatshop as a "choice." What do you think of this characterization? Is it accurate? Is it fair? In one or two paragraphs, explain whether you think people who work in sweatshops choose to do so and whether you think closing sweatshops would help or hurt such workers.

Chapter 3

How Should the United States Protect Human Rights?

Eileen Chamberlain Donahoe, the US representative to the United Nations Human Rights Council, works through the UN to promote human rights internationally.

The United States Must Emphasize Human Rights Protection in China

Steven Phillips

"Human rights must remain a significant part of America's China policy."

In the following viewpoint Steven Phillips argues that the United States must emphasize greater human rights protection in China. China has a reputation for abusing human rights—the government practices censorship, its people are not free to worship, and they are denied other freedoms and rights. Phillips contends that as the United States pursues its relationship with China, it must address these human rights violations. Currently, the United States ignores many of China's abuses or addresses them in an understated way for fear of jeopardizing talks on other issues, such as the environment or the economy. But Phillips maintains that making human rights a significant part of America's policy toward China has multiple long-term benefits for both countries.

Phillips is a professor of history at Towson University in Maryland.

AS YOU READ, CONSIDER THE FOLLOWING QUESTIONS:
1. What kinds of issues do US leaders focus on when engaging Chinese leaders, according to the author?
2. Who is Chen Guangcheng, as mentioned by Phillips?
3. What does the phrase "soft power" mean, as used by the author?

President Barack Obama's China policy combines deterrence and engagement, but it gives insufficient attention to human rights. Since early 2009, when Secretary of State Hillary Clinton [2009–2013] noted that human rights "can't interfere" with other aspects of Sino-American relations, the administration has tried to avoid public discussion of the issue.

United States Cannot Ignore Chinese Human Rights

Over the past year [2011–2012], the Obama administration has increased attention and resources devoted to East Asia. Expanded military cooperation with Australia and the Philippines, a robust Japanese-American defense relationship, and enhanced naval and air forces in the region illustrate Washington's efforts to counter China's growing assertiveness and military power. Human rights, however, has been left out of this regional effort.

Attempts at engagement were on display last week [May 2012] when Secretary of State Hillary Clinton, Secretary of the Treasury Timothy Geithner and a host of high-level American officials traveled to China for the fourth round of the Strategic and Economic Dialogue. Each side promised to increase economic integration, scientific exchanges and environmental cooperation. Human rights have not been a significant part of these meetings. When the two sides do discuss human rights, the talks are held separately and are led by lower-level officials.

The Obama administration's strategy was nearly overwhelmed by Chen Guangcheng, a blind, self-taught lawyer from Shandong Province. Because of Mr. Chen's efforts to obtain justice for the victims of China's coercive family planning policies, local officials harassed, confined and brutalized him and his family for years. Beijing tacitly approved these actions. Mr. Chen made a daring escape to the United States Embassy, and his plight brought renewed attention to human rights violations in China. American and Chinese diplomats rushed to forge an agreement to ensure Mr. Chen's safety prior to the dialogue meetings. The agreement did not provide adequate protection for Mr. Chen, and the resulting recriminations only increased tensions.

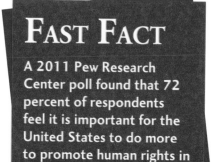

FAST FACT

A 2011 Pew Research Center poll found that 72 percent of respondents feel it is important for the United States to do more to promote human rights in China.

Now, a new agreement may enable Mr. Chen and his family to leave China to study in the United States. Whether Washington likes it or not, the fate of Mr. Chen and other dissidents now dominates Congressional, media and public attention.

Addressing Human Rights Has Many Benefits

For several reasons, human rights must remain a significant part of America's China policy:

- First, enhancing America's military capabilities in the region may be necessary, but it is not sufficient. Simply reacting to China's military build-up will create an arms race that no one wants. Through greater attention to human rights, the United States can focus on what it is for, rather than whom it is against. Promotion of human rights can be one non-military way to promote regional cooperation.
- Second, when Americans vacillate on human rights, it fosters the idea that the United States and its ideals are in decline. The United States is one of the few nations willing and able to openly

rebuke China on human rights or other issues. If support for human rights in China is lukewarm in Washington, it will become almost non-existent elsewhere. Human rights should be a key component of American "soft power."

- Third, when the political party in power (whether Republicans or Democrats) gives short-shrift to human rights concerns, it invites criticism from the human rights community and the opposition party. Particularly in an election year, partisan conflict over human rights reduces American credibility on this issue, as many in China can portray American concerns as nothing more than domestic political posturing. A better strategy would be for the administration to show that it is serious about this issue and to seek a bipartisan consensus.

- Fourth, a more systematic high-level dialogue on human right issues in China could help prevent the sort of rushed, ad hoc, negotiations that have made the Chen Guangcheng incident so potentially explosive. China's President and Communist Party

The Obama administration's human rights policy toward China was tested when Chinese dissident Chen Guangcheng (shown) escaped to the American embassy in Beijing.

chief Hu Jintao and its probable future leader, Xi Jinping, will probably object to any effort to raise the profile of human rights concerns. However, the risk that the next dissident seeking United States protection will spark a crisis makes it worthwhile to push this issue. The onus should be on Beijing to reject these talks.

A Better Long-Term Relationship

Secretary Clinton should include discussions on human rights in the annual Strategic and Economic Dialogue meetings. Further, she should lead these discussions. Greater attention to human rights will provoke short-term anger from the Beijing government, but it will garner long-term benefits. China's leaders will have a more realistic understanding of American views, and the United States can show its allies that China policy is built on more than military power and immediate economic benefits.

EVALUATING THE AUTHOR'S ARGUMENTS:

Steven Phillips, the author of this viewpoint, is an American college professor. Zhao Shanchu, author of the following viewpoint, is a Chinese academic. How do you think their differing backgrounds inform their opinions on this topic? Does knowing each author's background influence your opinion of their arguments? If so, how? If not, why not?

The United States Should Not Emphasize Human Rights Protection in China[1]

Zhao Shanchu

"It is neither fair nor logical . . . to focus on a few individual [human rights] cases while ignoring the remarkable achievements made by 1.3 billion Chinese people."

Zhao Shanchu is an international-relations scholar who lives in Beijing, China. In the following viewpoint, he argues that the United States oversteps its bounds when it lectures China on human rights. For one, he says, China has made vast improvements in human rights. Chinese people now enjoy greater democracy, greater protection of minorities, and greater protection by a stronger legal system, he contends. China retains the right to crack down on people who plot to overthrow the government or who rebel in ways that threaten the state, he argues, adding that no country, including the United States, tolerates this kind of treason. Shanchu maintains that people who claim to be human rights defenders are

1. The title of this article was added for the purposes of this book.

actually criminals and deserve to be treated as such. He warns that misrepresenting the state of human rights in China will not improve relations between his country and the United States.

AS YOU READ, CONSIDER THE FOLLOWING QUESTIONS:
1. Who is Gary Locke, as mentioned by the author?
2. According to Shanchu, what is a more accurate way to characterize people who have been dubbed "human rights defenders" in China?
3. What is the author trying to prove by citing sections 2383 and 2385 of the US criminal code?

All countries, developed and developing alike, are attaching unprecedented importance to human rights nowadays. Reports on human rights issues often grab headlines.

Because of the fast development, any news related to China may attract much attention from the international community. When someone mentions "human rights" and "China" in the same breath, it naturally draws eyeballs. Therefore, playing up so-called human rights issues in China has become a shortcut for certain Western media and politicians to grab attention and make a name for themselves.

The Truth About China

US Ambassador to China Gary Locke has attracted attention recently. On the eve of assuming his duties in China, he claimed that he would "raise human rights issues and individual cases with Chinese government officials at the highest levels". After coming to Beijing, he has pointed fingers at China's human rights situation on several occasions. He has even said that human rights climate in China is "getting worse" days ago [in January 2012].

Maybe that's part of Locke's routine job. But he should know China more than other Westerners in a more objective way. He should have a better idea about whether livelihoods of the Chinese people in the past decades have improved or deteriorated, and whether the rights they enjoy have expanded or narrowed. He should be aware of the fact that "the State respects and preserves human rights" has been incorporated into China's Constitution and the protection and promotion of human rights have been part of the overall strategy of national economic and social development.

Many Human Rights Gains in China

China has taken remarkable strides in many aspects over the years. The legal system of human rights protection has developed. Democracy and rule of law has improved. The rights and interests of all ethnic groups are safeguarded, and poverty alleviation efforts strengthened. All these developments deserve credit if viewed in a fair manner. However, it's really regrettable to see that Locke has turned a blind eye to China's great achievements and dwelled on tiny issues and a few people and made such inappropriate remarks.

Some Westerners claimed that they were "deeply concerned" over the so-called crackdown on several "human rights defenders" in China. In fact, the "human rights defenders" they referred to are people that breached Chinese laws and regulations. Every government shoulders the responsibility to maintain social stability and safeguard the rule of law. It is the obligation of the Chinese judicial authorities to punish those who plot to subvert the State and jeopardize national security. It is a matter of China's judicial sovereignty.

If certain Westerners insist on associating it with human rights, then how will they interpret section 2383 regarding the crime of rebellion and insurrection as well as section 2385 regarding the crime of advocating overthrow of government in Chapter 115 of the US Code? How will they interpret the cases, dealt [with] by the US judicial authorities, of inciting confrontation between US citizens and the government over issues of military service and military operations abroad in the last century?

US ambassador to China Gary Locke (pictured) caused controversy by stating his intent to raise human rights issues with the Chinese government upon his appointment.

It is neither fair nor logical for certain Westerners to focus on a few individual cases while ignoring the remarkable achievements made by 1.3 billion Chinese people.

The Wrong Way to Improve US-China Relations

Recently, several incidents have occurred in the US, too. Western politicians and media that have always boasted that they fly the flags of freedom of speech were silent on this. They tried hard to play down the influence of the incidents. Here come questions: How to balance the relations between maintaining social order and protecting the lawful rights of every citizen? How to avoid a double standard on democracy and freedom? Every country should make self-reflections on these questions.

If Locke could look at China's human rights progress in an objective and fair way, he would better enhance mutual trust between China and the US.

EVALUATING THE AUTHOR'S ARGUMENTS:

In this viewpoint Zhao Shanchu argues that every state has the right to defend itself against criminals who plot against the government. In what ways might a state defend itself against plots, but in doing so violate human rights? In what ways might a state defend itself against plots, but in doing so protect human rights? Are there cases in which a state rightfully should feel threatened, or cases in which a state would inappropriately feel threatened? Discuss these issues in three to five paragraphs and give at least one example of each scenario.

Viewpoint 3

The United States Should Go to War to Protect Human Rights

Kurt Volker

"What is the magic number [of deaths] that will finally prompt the international community to act in Syria?"

In the following viewpoint Kurt Volker argues that the United States should go to war to defend human rights. He discusses how civil war has raged in Syria since March 2011, as opposition to the regime of Bashar al-Assad has grown exponentially. To keep his grip on power, Assad has used brutal tactics to violate his people's rights, including dropping cluster bombs and Scud missiles on areas populated by civilians. Such tactics are in violation of international law and have claimed the lives of more than forty thousand people as of November 2012. As of December 2013, the United States had declined to intervene in the conflict, however. Volker brings up other conflicts in which America's hesitation to act cost thousands of lives—and the longer it waited, the more people died. In these conflicts, Americans have looked back and regretted taking so long to intervene.

Volker contends that Syria should not be another one of these situations and holds it up as an example of when it is appropriate to go to war to defend human rights and lives.

Volker is a former US ambassador to the North Atlantic Treaty Organization (NATO). He is a senior fellow at the Center for Transatlantic Relations at the Johns Hopkins University School of Advanced International Studies.

AS YOU READ, CONSIDER THE FOLLOWING QUESTIONS:
1. What does the phrase "leading from behind" mean as used by Volker in this viewpoint?
2. What happened in July 1995 in Srebrenica, as reported by the author?
3. What does Volker say is the most regrettable international human rights tragedy?

President [Barack] Obama was on the right track this week [April 2012] when he announced a new effort to monitor global hot spots and prevent mass atrocities before they happen.

But what about daily atrocities unfolding now in Syria—where a UN-brokered cease-fire is growing weaker by the day and the world refrains from intervening to stop the violence?

A Lesson from History

In this case, a history lesson from the Bosnian War is worth remembering. On May 1–2, 1993, negotiators at a resort outside of Athens reached agreement on the "Vance-Owen peace plan" [negotiated by former US secretary of state Cyrus Vance and former British foreign minister David Owen] aimed at ending Bosnia's civil war. The plan required Bosnian Serbs to stop shelling Sarajevo, where Bosnian Muslims were under a year-long siege. The catch: Western military force might be required to implement the cease-fire.

In 1993, US Secretary of State Warren Christopher began consultations with European allies to gauge their level of support for military force. But instead of assuring that the United States was prepared to lead the charge, he asked allies whether they were prepared to implement the plan, without committing the US either way. ("Leading from behind" is what one might call this today.)

Sensing the US was not prepared to lead implementation—President [Bill] Clinton had won the election just six months earlier on the slogan, "It's the economy, stupid"—allies demurred.

Thousands Died Until the US Intervened

Within a week, the Bosnian Serb parliament rejected the plan, and shelling resumed. The war raged for two more years, with the Bosnian enclaves of Gorazde and Zepa falling to ethnic Serb forces, their majority Bosniak populations forcibly expelled.

Then, in July 1995 in Srebrenica, Bosnian Serbs murdered more [than] 7,000 Bosniaks in one, systematic slaughter. It was at that point that the West finally acted. To his lasting credit, President Clinton then determined that the US would lead. NATO [North Atlantic Treaty Organization] used air power to suppress Bosnian Serb attacks on Sarajevo, and within months had committed to military implementation of the Dayton peace accord, driven to conclusion by American über-diplomat Richard Holbrooke. By December 1995, some 60,000 NATO troops were en route to Bosnia to implement the peace plan, 20,000 of them American.

What was the difference between May 1993 and July 1995? In terms of Western implementation—nothing. We did in 1995 roughly what we would have done in 1993, had we acted. But in terms of human cost—tens of thousands of lives were lost.

Action Saves Lives

And that is the key lesson. Eventually, the West was willing to act. But it took a "catalyst" of thousands of lives lost in a single massacre to convince us to do what we could have done years before. Would it not have been better to have acted sooner and saved thousands of lives?

As we look back over recent decades, there have been a surprising number of mass-murder conflicts. Bosnia, Kosovo, Saddam Hussein's attacks on the Kurds in Iraq, and Libya, to name a few. In each case, outside powers intervened at some point to stop the killing. The results—while imperfect—nonetheless saved thousands of lives and laid the groundwork for future settlements.

Death and Suffering in Syria

As of November 2012, more than forty thousand people had been killed by Syria's ongoing civil war, and tens of thousands had fled the country. Some argued the human rights abuses were so dire, international intervention was warranted. The death toll topped one hundred thousand just eight months later, in July 2013.

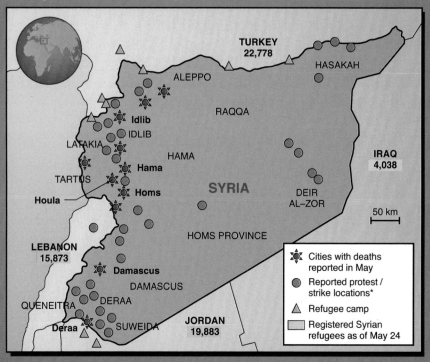

Taken from: United Nations Institute for Training and Research, UNITAR's Operational Satellite Applications Programme (UNOSAT), Syrian Shuhada, United Nations High Commissioner for Refugees (UNHCR), US Department of State.

And of all these recent conflicts, which is the one we regret the most? Rwanda, where some 800,000 people were killed and the West did nothing.

This is the perspective one must bring to the conflict now raging in Syria.

What Is the Magic Number?
Nearly all the arguments against intervention in Syria have merit. It is difficult. The Syrian military is strong. Outside powers such as

Iran and Russia are engaged. The local politics are complicated. What comes after intervention? Who are the people we would help? What if a revolution is hijacked?

Sound familiar? It should. These are the same arguments, with a few modifications, that were heard before the interventions in Libya, Kosovo, Kurdish-Iraq, and Bosnia. And after hearing all of them, and seeing the killing continue, we should ask ourselves, "and then what?"

Imagine that after the shelling of Horns, after the shelling of Damascus suburbs, after everything we have seen over the past year, some new slaughter takes place. Imagine 5,000 people killed in one

Rescue teams recover bodies of those killed in fighting in Damascus, Syria. The huge death toll and constant violations of human rights by the Syrian regime have resulted in a call by some Westerners to intervene in the civil war.

fell swoop. Or 7,000. Or 9,000. It's happened before. In 1982, Bashar al-Assad's father sent the military to the city of Hama to put down an armed insurrection, killing at least 10,000 people.

What is the magic number that will finally prompt the international community to act in Syria?

Saving Lives Is Right and Possible

The moral principles arguing for intervention are already known: The Syrian government is engaged in a systematic campaign of mass murder, seeking to kill anyone who dares oppose it, in order to re-establish firm control. The state of Syria has a monopoly of force—in the military, police, intelligence services, and secret police. The people are standing up with great valor—but little capacity—to oppose such tyranny. Over 9,000 people have been killed—though over a year's time, not at once.

How to intervene? There's no easy answer, but having no answer is even worse. On the political side, we have to assume that Russia will block any intervention resolution in the UN Security

FAST FACT

As of July 2013, the United Nations estimated that at least one hundred thousand people had been killed by the ongoing civil war in Syria, many of them by the government.

Council. And so the world would need to be prepared to act without one—just as in Kosovo in 1999.

Participation by regional states is important—particularly Turkey, Saudi Arabia, Qatar, and the United Arab Emirates. Given France's post-imperial history in Syria and Lebanon, it is better to have France (and, for that matter, Britain) on board a liberating intervention.

On the mechanics, it would require suppressing Syria's offensive capabilities and air defenses and jamming communications. A "safe zone" would need to be established inside the country, which would allow for unfettered distribution of humanitarian relief and create a space where the opposition could organize and receive further training and support (think Benghazi in Libya).

America Will Not Want to Look Back and Ask Why

This is a difficult and dangerous course, surpassed only by the difficult and dangerous course we are already traveling.

What is missing, therefore, is not an understanding of the case for intervention, or even a means to intervene, but a "catalyst" that justifies and forces action. If that catalyst occurs, the US and others might act. And then America and its friends should ask themselves why they did not act sooner, and prevent the very catastrophe that spurred them into action.

> **EVALUATING THE AUTHOR'S ARGUMENTS:**
>
> Kurt Volker and Brendan O'Neill (author of the following viewpoint) disagree on whether it is appropriate to go to war to defend human rights. What do you think? Is there an international humanitarian crisis to which you would be willing to commit US troops? What would that crisis be like? What kinds of human rights violations might make it worth it? Select a real event from history to make your argument.

The United States Should Not Go to War to Protect Human Rights

Brendan O'Neill

"All Western interventions of the past 15 years have been 'humanitarian'—and that is why all have been such unmitigated, bloody disasters."

War is not justified, even to protect human rights, argues Brendan O'Neill in the following viewpoint. He agrees that there are places in the world in which unspeakable human rights violations are committed—for example, in Libya, where former dictator Muammar Gaddafi killed and repressed hundreds of thousands of people before his death in 2011. But O'Neill says going to war to stop people like Gaddafi does not make sense. Moral military efforts tend to lack direction, purpose, and end up being very protracted, causing even more death than they initially had claimed to prevent. Furthermore, they are subjective: What one nation claims to be a morally justified war might be very different than what another nation claims to be a morally justified war. To O'Neill, there are neither good, humanitarian wars, nor bad, inappropriate wars—war is war, and people die and lose rights whenever war is undertaken. He concludes that it is selfish, narcissistic, and misguided for the United States and other Western countries to start wars to protect human rights.

Brendan O'Neill is editor of *Spiked,* a British newsmagazine.

AS YOU READ, CONSIDER THE FOLLOWING QUESTIONS:
1. What is the "Chicago Doctrine," as described by O'Neill?
2. What does the term "axis of evil" mean as used by the author?
3. According to O'Neill, what is the difference between a humanitarian and a "neo-con"?

They're back. Having spent the past 10 years pretending to be anti-war—describing the attack on Iraq as 'criminal' and the war in Afghanistan as 'a trifle ill-judged'—the liberal and left-wing set that originally invented the idea of 'humanitarian warfare' in the 1990s are once more at the forefront of public debate. They've cast off the anti-imperialist garb that they temporarily donned to make their disappointment with [former British prime minister Tony] Blair and their snobbish disdain for [former American president George W.] Bush appear principled, to reveal that, underneath, there lurk the same old laptop bombardiers keen to visit their moralistic fury upon some wayward nation. This time they have Libya in their sights.

War and Moralism Do Not Mix

The speed with which observers who attacked Blair and Bush over Iraq have lined up behind [British prime minister David] Cameron and [US president Barack] Obama over Libya is remarkable. Deputy British prime minister Nick Clegg says his war on Libya is a 'different scenario from Iraq'; where Iraq was a product of the 'trigger-happy policies' of Blair's 'vigilantism', the bombing of Libya is '[United Nations (UN)] sanctioned and driven by humanitarian concerns'. More akin to Kosovo 1999 than Iraq 2003, 'it is *liberal* interventionism', says Clegg. This sentiment is echoed across the serious press that was so critical of the 'cowboy' Iraq venture. 'In the case of Libya, the principle [of humanitarianism] stands as clear as ever', says one columnist. It will no doubt be of great comfort to Libyans to know that their deaths are occurring in the name of 'humanitarian principles' rather than 'vigilantism'.

These anti-war critics turned pro-war cheerleaders might have no shame and few principles. But they do have a point. The bombing of Libya *is* a 'humanitarian war'—and that is what makes it so terrifying. For 'humanitarian warfare' is, if anything, even worse than yesteryear's Western invasions of the Third World in the name of territory, stuff or realpolitik. Driven more by moralism than by political calculations, underpinned by childlike assumptions about good and evil, utterly disconnected from the realm of geopolitical interests or gain, 'humanitarian intervention' is extraordinarily unpredictable and destabilising. It makes even the crimes of colonialism look rational in comparison.

No Good War or Bad War—Only War

The first thing that should be shot down is the nonsense notion that there's a world of difference between the wars cheered by liberals (Kosovo in 1999, Libya today) and the wars led by the Bush administration (Afghanistan in 2001, Iraq in 2003). Reading recent commentary, you could be forgiven for thinking that there are two, implacably divergent camps of foreign interventionists, one of which is good and pure (the 'humanitarians') and one of which is wicked and self-interested (the 'neoconservatives'). This is one of the most fantastic fallacies in modern political discourse. In reality, the humanitarians and neocons share precisely the same urge: to escape the drab domestic sphere by acting out battles between good and evil in the international sphere. And they share precisely the same assumption: that they have the right to interfere in other states' affairs.

Indeed, the 'neocon' ventures in Afghanistan and Iraq were underpinned by what was known as the 'Chicago doctrine'—a speech given by then 'humanitarian' Tony Blair in Chicago in 1999 in which, to the whooping and high-fiving of liberal hacks everywhere, he outlined the circumstances in which the West might launch military ventures. He called for a shift away from the Cold War era emphasis on the sanctity of state sovereignty and towards a new willingness to intervene in 'regimes that are undemocratic and engaged in barbarous acts'. His call for a rethinking of the overly legalistic postwar set-up—which was championed in [a London] *Observer* editorial that said 'the UN's imprimatur cannot be the sole trigger for international action to right an obvious wrong'—is known to have influenced Bush and his cronies, then waiting in the wings. It's just that where Blair's demand that we move beyond the obsession with sovereign integrity was widely described as 'brave', when the Bush administration suggested likewise they were denounced as 'law-breakers'.

Saving People Is Narcissistic and Misguided

Whether they are saving Kosovo Albanians from evil [Slobodan] Milosevic, Afghan women from the evil Taliban or Benghazians from 'mad dog' [Mu'ammar] Gaddafi, the interventions of both the 'humanitarians' and the 'neocons' have been narcissistic and highly moralised, in which they themselves play the role of knights on white chargers and the people of Third World have at best a walk-on part as pathetic victims in need of rescue. Everyone mocked Bush when he used terms like 'Axis of Evil' in relation to wicked foreign states and somewhat apologetically said 'some worry that it is undiplomatic or impolite to speak the language of right and wrong. . .' Yet it was Blair and his 'humanitarian' cheerleaders who first supermoralised international affairs, with Blair describing NATO's [North Atlantic Treaty Organization's] war on Serbia in 1999 as 'a battle between good and evil; between civilisation and barbarity; between democracy and dictatorship'.

The distinction made between 'humanitarians' and 'neocons' is utterly false. It is a case of linguistic gymnastics, where the ultimate aim is to distance liberals from the barbarism of the Iraq War. Keen to wash their hands of that mayhem, which was in fact set in motion by their zealous moralisation of the international sphere in the 1990s and their complicity in the development of a doctrine that pushed aside legal norms in favour of doing what was 'right' against 'evil', they branded it as 'neocon'

> **FAST FACT**
>
> In 2012 a Pew Research Center poll found that 64 percent of Americans believed that countries that receive aid from the United States end up resenting America, whereas only 29 percent disagreed.

in order to present it as alien, strange, a mistake, 'nothing to do with me, guvnor'. In truth, it had everything to do with them. All Western interventions of the past 15 years have been 'humanitarian'—and that is why all have been such unmitigated, bloody disasters.

In Chicago in 1999 British prime minister Tony Blair (shown) outlined the circumstances in which the West might launch military interventions without UN approval against "regimes that are undemocratic and engaged in barbarous acts," which has come to be called the Chicago Doctrine.

A War-Weary West

The wars in Iraq and Afghanistan killed thousands of soldiers, cost billions of dollars, and left Americans, British, and other people who fought in them war weary. After years of war, many are reluctant to get involved in a humanitarian military effort if there is no direct or immediate threat to their nation.

	Iraq Coalition Military Fatalities, by Year			
Year	United States	United Kingdom	Other	Total
2003	486	53	41	580
2004	849	22	35	906
2005	846	23	28	897
2006	823	29	21	873
2007	904	47	10	961
2008	314	4	4	322
2009	149	1	0	150
2010	60	0	0	60
2011	54	0	0	54
2012	1	0	0	1
Total	**4,486**	**179**	**139**	**4,804**

	Afghanistan Coalition Military Fatalities, by Year			
Year	United States	United Kingdom	Other	Total
2001	12	0	0	12
2002	49	3	18	70
2003	48	0	10	58
2004	52	1	7	60
2005	99	1	31	131
2006	98	39	54	191
2007	117	42	73	232
2008	155	51	89	295
2009	317	108	96	521
2010	499	103	109	711
2011	418	46	102	566
2012	307	44	45	396
Total	**2,171**	**438**	**634**	**3,243**

Taken from: Casualties.org, December 2012.

Moral Wars Are Selfish and Lack Direction

The key problem with the 'humanitarian' outlook is its downgrading of old-style political interests in favour of pursuing the moral imperative. That is, the thing that its supporters claim as its virtue—its alleged selflessness—is the very thing that makes it so destructive. This is not to say that wars in pursuit of a clear political goal or territorial gain, with which history is littered, are, by contrast, good. But those old interventions were at least *anchored*, rooted and directed by goals and endgames, giving rise to an instinct on the part of the Western invaders to know something about the territory they were invading, to cultivate Western-friendly political movements, and to have an end-point in mind. In contrast, the humanitarians' aim is to display their moral righteousness against an entity they have judged to be evil, and thus they're more likely simply to launch PR [public relations] stunts in foreign lands, whether 'shock and awe' in Iraq or 'Odyssey Dawn' in Libya. The consequences of such stunts are highly unpredictable.

Back when he was a 'humanitarian', and thus loved by the smart set, rather than a 'neocon', and thus despised by the smart set, Tony Blair said that NATO's bombardment of Serbia in 1999 was 'not a war for territory but for values. . . . [it is] a battle between good and evil'. He unwittingly echoed [former Iranian leader] Ayatollah Khomeini, who in 1984 said of Iran's war with Iraq: 'This is not a war for territory. It is a war between Islam and blasphemy.' Blair's post-modern, post-territorial injection of Ayatollah-style religiosity into international affairs has been embraced by the neocons in relation to Iraq: this is 'not a war for wealth', they told us, but 'for hearts and minds'. On Libya, Obama has spoken a little bit about America's national interests—primarily as an assurance that Washington won't commit ground troops or spend too much money—but he says these interests are outweighed by the moral imperative to 'act on behalf of what's right'. This self-conscious elbowing aside of national interests in preference of pursuing values has given rise to an international sphere bereft of rules and dangerously morally charged.

The humanitarians' moralisation of other people's conflicts, their treatment of everything in simplistic terms of good and evil, has huge potential to destabilise countries further and to up the military ante. Many claim that the West had to intervene in Libya to prevent a massacre in Benghazi, yet the intervention itself has created the perfect breeding ground for intensified violence. After all, when a political conflict is redefined as a battle between good and evil, as an apocalyptic event, where is the scope for a ceasefire or negotiation?

It Is Not for the West to Decide

The international isolation of Gaddafi's regime, the description of him as 'evil' (far more evil than those carrying out massacres in Bahrain apparently), creates a situation where he has little left to lose. Transformed into a pariah, he is starting to act like one, possibly deciding that to go out with all guns blazing would be preferable to ending up in [the International Criminal Court at] The Hague. What's more, the West's treatment of the self-appointed leaders of the rebel movement as 'good', despite the fact that we know little about them, could ossify the Libyan uprising, handing the initiative to groups that remain largely mysterious but which have been anointed by kneejerk Western humanitarians as pure and decent representatives of the Libyan people. The history of humanitarian interventionism tells us that the transformation of relatively low-level civil conflicts into historic wars between evil men and their whiter-than-white opponents does nobody any good.

In terms of the so-called coalition in the West, its 'humanitarian' instincts mean that it has launched a war without leadership, without war aims, and without any tangible endpoint. Motored by the humanitarians' narcissistic desire, not to win territory or create pro-Western political movements, but simply to advertise their values of decency and morality, Cameron, [French president Nicolas] Sarkozy and Obama rushed into a bombing campaign without giving a second thought to what its consequences might be. This recklessness, this fatal rashness on the part of Western leaders, is a direct product of the 'humanitarian' outlook: the elevation of values over territorial ambition, of moralism over realpolitik, of narcissism over old-style political gain, creates a situation where wars are launched for effect, to send a message, with little analysis or intelligence about what might happen later. Libya has been transformed, not into the latest outpost of any kind of Western Empire, but into a stage for the amateur yet deadly dramatics of Western politicians and hacks desperately seeking moral momentum.

Jonathan Freedland at the [Manchester] *Guardian,* who supports the bombing, says the trouble with the intervention 'is not with the abstract principle but with the concrete practice': 'The effort is too rushed, with key operational decisions—including command—not fixed.' In fact, it is the very 'principles' of humanitarianism, its downgrading of realpolitik in favour of big, loud, fleeting displays of shallow Western moralism, which give rise to the confused practice. It was the humanitarian urge to 'do something' in Libya which led to a war where 'key operational decisions' were not made beforehand. It is in the very essence of 'humanitarianism' to rush into conflict zones, show off one's values, make things worse, and then leave and forget all about it.

That is why *spiked* is opposed to this doublespeak humanitarian war on Libya: because it is reckless, unpredictable, destructive, and it puts off further the day when ordinary Libyans, rather than those blindly picked by the West, might take command of their affairs.

EVALUATING THE AUTHOR'S ARGUMENTS:

Brendan O'Neill thinks it is hypocritical that the people who opposed going to war in Iraq and Afghanistan now want the United States and its allies to go to war in places like Libya and Syria. Given what you know about these wars, do you think there are differences between them? Explain your reasoning.

Viewpoint
5

The United States Should Give Humanitarian Aid to Enemy Countries

"Humanitarian aid decisions should be above politics."

Richard Weitz

The United States has a moral obligation to give humanitarian aid to suffering people even if their government is hostile toward the United States, argues Richard Weitz in the following viewpoint. He discusses the case of North Korea, which has for years been at odds with the United States and much of the international community for its insistence on developing nuclear weapons. North Korea is run by a brutal dictatorship that has little regard for its people; citizens routinely suffer from devastating famines because the government spends its money on maintaining its military rather than caring for civilians. In Weitz's opinion, North Koreans should not be punished because of their government. He thinks humanitarian aid should be divorced from politics—if people are suffering, they deserve help regardless of who happens to represent them. Furthermore, he warns that withholding aid from North Korea can make them unwilling to negotiate on weapons, worsen their refugee problem, and critically weaken the people so they are unable to resist their dictator. He concludes that giving aid is the best way to make progress with North Korea and can strengthen sectors of Korean society poised to oppose the regime.

Weitz is director of the Center for Political-Military Analysis and a senior fellow at the Hudson Institute. He frequently comments on international affairs in the *International Herald Tribune,* the *Guardian,* the *Wall Street Journal,* and other publications.

AS YOU READ, CONSIDER THE FOLLOWING QUESTIONS:
1. How much food aid does Weitz say the United States has given to North Korea?
2. What have aid workers seen North Korean children eat to stay alive, according to Weitz?
3. Who is Robert King, as mentioned by the author?

The [Barack] Obama administration has been deliberating for months now [in 2011] whether to resume food aid to North Korea. And, with North Korean representatives now being joined by international relief organizations in citing the threat of famine, there would seem to be an easy case for resuming assistance. Or at least it would be easy—if it were virtually any other country in the world.

The Tricky Case of Aid to North Korea
The US government has traditionally been the largest source of international food assistance to North Korea, supplying almost $800 million of food aid to the country. Almost all of this was flown through the UN [United Nations] World Food Programme [WFP]—until [North Korean capital city] Pyongyang's decision a few years back to refuse to accept the WFP's strict conditions led to a suspension of deliveries.

And, although conditions aren't as bad as during the mid-1990s famine, when perhaps a million people died due to a lack of food, there's general agreement that most North Koreans are suffering from insufficient food consumption. Indeed, missions from several US and other foreign relief organizations have seen starving children eating grass.

People Should Not Be Punished for Their Government

Still, there's general agreement that the North Korean government is almost entirely responsible for the famine and other calamities plaguing its people. The government's skewed economic and political policies have resulted in its prioritizing defence spending and other spending categories besides food, sanitation, health care, and essential public services. Its restrictions on economic activity, combined with the political criteria that govern the government's centrally controlled food distribution system, has also prevented food from reaching the neediest people even when it's available.

For example, the country's best products, as well as imported luxuries, often go to the elites in charge of the country's security forces and other institutions. Unlike many former communist countries, the North Korean leadership has declined to introduce major reforms in what remains essentially a Stalinist-style command economy for fear of undermining this patronage system and allowing market freedoms that might encourage greater demands for political liberties.

Most recently, the North Korean government mismanaged a comprehensive currency reform introduced in 2009. The policy ended up impoverishing many North Koreans by wiping out their savings, depriving them of the means to purchase adequate food and other goods. Meanwhile, last winter [2010–2011] was much colder and longer than usual, while this summer saw heavy rainfall. The elevated international prices for oil and food have reduced the volumes of these goods that North Korea is buying for imports. Although like other countries North Korea suffers from floods, crop and livestock diseases and other natural disasters, its government's policies have left many North Koreans excessively vulnerable to such calamities.

Of course, the country's culpability alone wouldn't prevent the United States and other countries from providing assistance. After all, they've given help to needy inhabitants of the Soviet Union, Sudan, and many other people suffering due to government mismanagement. These people typically have little say in their governments' policies. In addition, there's a widespread principle that humanitarian aid decisions should be above politics.

North Korea Is Difficult

But many people consider North Korea to be an especially odious recipient of international assistance. Its government's foreign policies are as horrific as its domestic practices, and the country is presently the regime most clearly in violation of its non-proliferation commitments. Not only has it regularly peddled nuclear and ballistic missile

American wheat is off-loaded at a port in North Korea. Although North Korea is considered a brutal dictatorship, many think humanitarian aid to the nation should not be stopped because it may jeopardize negotiations on nuclear weapons.

technologies on international markets to rogue actors, but Pyongyang has already tested two nuclear explosive devices and is trying to perfect a long-range ballistic missile capable of reaching the United States.

Nor is North Korea an easy government to work with. The government restricts the number and movement of aid workers, prohibits Korean-speakers from assisting in the distribution, and has shown little gratitude for the help. Due to the lack of a free market, some collective farms underreport their food production and sell the hidden surpluses on the black market. There are also legitimate fears that, even if the government doesn't divert the aid, then the North Korean authorities will use any assistance to free up resources for other malign purposes, such as supporting their military.

The fact is that as with many policy questions regarding North Korea, there are no good options regarding the food aid question. But on balance, the best course would be for the United States and perhaps the South Korean government to modify their policies and render the food relief.

Problems Caused By *Lack* of Aid

South Koreans for their part need to consider the additional problems they will face following reunification if the North Koreans that join a reunified country suffer from stunted physical and mental growth, vitamin and iron deficiencies, and increased diseases due to chronic maternal and child malnutrition. These problems are already evident in the large number of Northern refugees who flee to the South.

Furthermore, both Americans and South Koreans should consider that, while the current suspension of engagement with North Korea may be tolerable for another year, when the North Korean leadership will be focused on its political succession process, the stalemate is

North Korea Is Not Viewed Positively by Americans

Americans have an overwhelmingly unfavorable opinion of North Korea because of ongoing tensions with the regime. Still, some separate government-level conflict from the needs of the people, who routinely suffer from famine and lack of supplies.

Question: What is your overall opinion of _____? Is it very favorable, mostly favorable, mostly unfavorable, or very unfavorable?

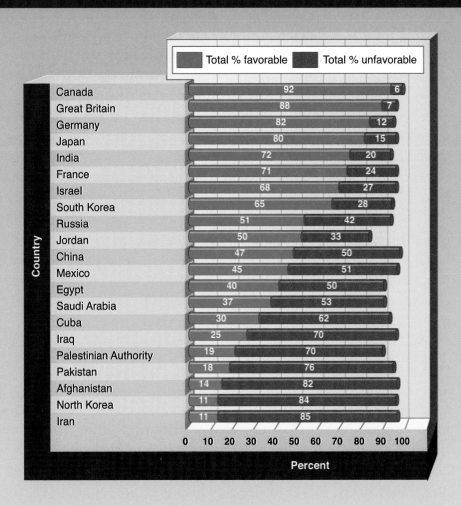

Country	Total % favorable	Total % unfavorable
Canada	92	6
Great Britain	88	7
Germany	82	12
Japan	80	15
India	72	20
France	71	24
Israel	68	27
South Korea	65	28
Russia	51	42
Jordan	50	33
China	47	50
Mexico	45	51
Egypt	40	50
Saudi Arabia	37	53
Cuba	30	62
Iraq	25	70
Palestinian Authority	19	70
Pakistan	18	76
Afghanistan	14	82
North Korea	11	84
Iran	11	85

Percent

Taken from: Gallup, February 2–5, 2011.

inherently unstable. Pyongyang could at any time resume testing its nuclear weapons and long-range ballistic missiles [it did so in 2013]. Together, these capabilities could render the continental United States vulnerable to a direct nuclear attack. And the risk that further North Korean provocations on the Peninsula will escalate into a major war have increased due to South Korea's new policy of retaliating more directly to further North Korean outrages.

Aid Can Lead to Talks and Security

The United States should therefore offer food assistance as a means of jump starting a dialogue with Pyongyang that eventually needs to extend to security issues. Official US policy is to separate humanitarian aid decisions from strategic considerations. In the words of the US special envoy for North Korean human rights issues, Robert King, 'The United States policy is that when we provide assistance, humanitarian assistance, it is based on need and no political consideration should be involved. That's the first condition.'

In practice, the United States and other governments have regularly used aid to induce Pyongyang to modify its domestic and foreign policies. Both the [George W.] Bush and Obama administrations have indicated they would continue this practice and provide a comprehensive aid package if North Korea dismantled its nuclear weapons programme in a completely verifiable manner. The [Myung-bak] Lee government [of South Korea] has made similar offers of comprehensive assistance in return for de-nuclearization.

Aid Can Strengthen North Korea

Of course, one needs to appreciate the limits of this approach. Foreign food aid may help re-launch talks, but it will not by itself lead to any major concessions or a long-term change in North Korean behaviour. But in addition to helping re-launch a necessary dialogue, a well-designed food assistance programme could help stimulate the growth of private markets in North Korea, which over time should weaken the regime's control over its people.

For these reasons, US officials should consider providing some aid even if [South Korea's capital] Seoul doesn't, though the United

States should respect a South Korean refusal to resume its own help—and South Korean officials should reciprocate and not consider a resumption of American aid as a breach of alliance solidarity. The recent dual aid ban is unusual and not necessarily a wise or sustainable policy.

> ## EVALUATING THE AUTHOR'S ARGUMENTS:
>
> To make his argument, Richard Weitz claims that giving aid can strengthen sectors of North Korean society that could be poised to oppose the regime, thus weakening it from the inside. How would Patrick M. Cronin and Abraham M. Denmark, the authors of the following viewpoint, likely respond to this claim? Sum up their likely position in two to three sentences, then state with which viewpoint you agree, and why.

To Feed, or Not to Feed

Patrick M. Cronin and Abraham M. Denmark

"Humanitarian assistance and food aid are no more than subsidies to sustain the reign of the Kim Family regime."

Giving humanitarian aid to nations led by hostile governments only perpetuates the problems of starvation and suffering, argue Patrick M. Cronin and Abraham M. Denmark in the following viewpoint. They contend that for years, North Korea has agreed to trade weapons and military technology for food, medicine, and other aid for its starving people. But North Koreans continue to build weapons in secret and siphon off the received aid, not to the people who need it, but to the military and elite ranks of the government. Cronin and Denmark say it is insane to continue this pointless process that exploits Americans' good will and generosity. If humanitarian aid cannot be guaranteed to reach the people who need it, it should not continue to be given. They maintain that the North Korean government will only change when it is truly pressured; continuing to supply it with humanitarian aid only keeps the problem in power.

Cronin is senior director of the Asia-Pacific Security Program at the Center for a New American Security (CNAS), where Denmark is a fellow.

1. What action contributed to North Korea's 2011 food shortage, according to the authors?
2. What, according to Cronin and Denmark, happened in the 1990s when the United States agreed to give food and fuel to North Korea in exchange for denuclearization?
3. What does the United Nations World Food Programme require of nations to which it gives aid, as reported by the authors?

The Obama administration has recently come under fire for standing by its decision to refuse North Korea emergency food aid, despite Pyongyang's requests for help and emerging reports of malnutrition within the DPRK (Democratic People's Republic of Korea—North Korea's formal name). Selig Harrison, writing in *The National Interest*, claims the administration's policy "simply adds to the deprivation of the North Korean masses in urban centers" and calls for "a long-term food aid commitment to Pyongyang in exchange for denuclearization concessions." Harrison specifically targets Assistant Secretary of State for East Asia and the Pacific Kurt Campbell; he blames Campbell for the administration's policies and for refusing to allow Harrison to convene a proposed discussion of U.S.–North Korean policy issues (in the interest of full disclosure, Campbell co-founded the Center for a New American Security, the home organization of the two authors).

While the decision to deny North Korea food aid at a time when malnutrition appears to be rising is certainly a painful one, the Obama administration is doing the right thing. It has been widely reported that any food aid that arrives in North Korea is diverted away from ordinary citizens and doled out to key constituents, especially in the military. It is precisely for this reason that Pyongyang refuses to allow aid workers the ability to conduct routine monitoring of humanitarian aid delivery. And it is precisely for this reason that the international humanitarian community insists on monitoring assistance, to ensure that emergency aid goes to those facing the humanitarian crisis. As presently controlled by arguably the world's most autocratic regime, humanitarian assistance and food aid are no more than subsidies to

Years of Aid and No Progress

The United States and other bodies have given massive amounts of aid to North Korea for more than fifteen years, but there has been little progress getting the regime to abandon its nuclear weapons program.

Calendar or Fiscal Year (FY)	Food Aid (per FY)		KEDO Assistance (per calendar yr; $ million)	6-Party Talks-Related Assistance (per FY; $ million)		Medical Supplies & Other (per FY; $ million)	Total ($ million)
	Metric Tons	Commodity Value ($ million)		Fuel Oil	Nuclear Disable-ment		
1995	0	0.00	9.50	–	–	0.20	9.70
1996	19,500	8.30	22.00	–	–	0.00	30.30
1997	177,000	52.40	25.00	–	–	5.00	82.40
1998	200,000	72.90	50.00	–	–	0.00	122.90
1999	695,194	222.10	65.10		–	0.00	287.20
2000	265,000	74.30	64.40	–	–	0.00	138.70
2001	350,000	58.07	74.90	–	–	0.00	132.97
2002	207,000	50.40	90.50	–	–	0.00	140.90
2003	40,200	25.48	2.30	–	–	0.00	27.78
2004	110,000	36.30	0.00	–	–	0.10	36.40
2005	25,000	5.70	–	–	–	–	5.70
2006	0	0.00	–	–	–	0.00	0.00
2007	0	0.00	–	25.00	20.00	0.10	45.10
2008	148,270	93.70	–	106.00	25.00	0.00	224.70
2009	21,000	5.60	–	15.00	–	4.00	24.60
2010	–	2.90	–	–	–	0.60	3.50
2011	–	–	–	–	–	0.90	0.90
Total	2,258,164	708.15	403.70	146.00	45.00	10.90	1,313.75

Taken from: Congressional Research Service (CRS) from US Agency for International Development (USAID); US Department of Agriculture; State Department; KEDO (Korean Peninsula Energy Development Organization).

sustain the reign of the Kim Family regime. For those of us who are proud of America's generosity when it comes to humanitarian aid, we would far prefer that our assistance went to others in need rather than to have it stolen by North Korea's elite.

Americans should also keep in mind that the plight of the North Korean people is not simply an act of nature or the result of too little outside assistance but directly and indirectly caused by the decisions of its government. Wanton mismanagement, near-perfect isolation, and a reckless lack of investment by the government in Pyongyang is the root cause of its people's poverty. Kim Jong-Il has consistently spurned South Korean, American, Chinese, and other economic models of sustainable economic development. To be sure, North Korea flirted with some economic reforms, but in the end the regime tightly circumscribed their ability to create sustainable markets. Indeed, a recent report in South Korean media pointed out that last year's [2010's] harvest in the North was among the best in two decades, and that food shortage is being caused by government and military hoarding in preparation for 2012, when Pyongyang plans to declare itself a "powerful and prosperous nation."

Today, food relief is more like medical IVs that provide a direct infusion into the regime's leadership and elite. For instance, among the more than 45,000 North Korean workers allowed to work in the Kaesong Industrial District run by South Korea, the workers are all from elite members of the Korean Workers' Party, one of the reasons Pyongyang keeps the factories running even during times of tension, because the benefits go directly to Kim Jong-Il and members of the top one percent of North Korea's government. Until North Korean leaders change their policies, the DPRK will be perennially incapable of feeding its own people. Pyongyang understands this very well, yet has not made any serious move to reverse its fortunes.

Furthermore, Selig Harrison's proposal for a long-term food aid commitment in exchange for denu-

> # FAST FACT
>
> In the 1990s North Korea promised to end its nuclear weapons program in exchange for food and fuel from the United States. According to the International Institute for Strategic Studies, North Korea accepted the supplies but secretly built nuclear weapons in violation of the agreement.

clearization concessions ignores North Korea's well-documented history of violating its promises and commitments. Indeed, it has become clear that as the United States transferred food and fuel to North Korea in exchange for denuclearization concessions in the 1990s as part of the Agreed Framework, North Korea was clandestinely building nuclear

North Korean soldiers parade during a holiday celebration. Some world leaders argue that humanitarian aid to North Korea only helps the military and government elites and never gets to the general populace.

weapons and their related infrastructure. Moreover, North Korea has already agreed to fully denuclearize itself; there is no reason why the United States should, in the words of Secretary of Defense Robert Gates, "buy the same horse twice." But that is precisely the negotiating gambit that North Korea has used time and again to extract concessions from the outside world in exchange for pretending to be serious about doing something this time. We must learn from the past.

Yet the North Korean people need not starve as Washington and Pyongyang attempt to stare one another down. Instead of a grand "food for nukes" bargain that mirrors past attempts that have left both sides feeling cheated, why not a simple agreement on North Korea's side to allow international aid workers to ensure that food delivered to the North Korean people ends up on their plates and not in a North Korean government warehouse? Surely, it must be easier for Pyongyang to allow foreign aid workers into the country than to abandon a nuclear program it has vigorously pursued since the 1970s. Lest critics think this unfair, this is what is required in all emergency food aid programs administered by the United Nations World Food Program.

Because Americans genuinely want to do good in the world, they are vulnerable to actors who would prefer to defraud the system. In Zimbabwe we found ways to work with civil society in order to minimize propping up the repugnant regime of Robert Mugabe. But in North Korea, there is no civil society; there are also no truly academic exchanges or free-thinking seminars. Washington must always remain open to dialogue, and we should never stop searching for a way to provide humanitarian assistance to those in need. Quite separate from the food issue, we may also need to "make the first move" in order to reinitiate a meaningful denuclearization process. But one thing we should not do is to feed Kim Jong-Il's military while his regime allows ordinary people to starve.

EVALUATING THE AUTHOR'S ARGUMENTS:

Both Richard Weitz (author of the previous viewpoint) and Patrick M. Cronin and Abraham M. Denmark agree that North Korea is led by a brutal dictatorship that violates the rights of its people. Yet they disagree on whether the United States should continue to give food aid to the country. After reading both articles, select one quote that you think best sums up the heart of each authors' argument. Then, state with which view you ultimately agree, and why.

Facts About Human Rights

Editor's note: These facts can be used in reports to add credibility when making important points or claims.

What Constitutes a Human Right

According to the Universal Declaration of Human Rights adopted by the United Nations in 1948, all human beings:

1. are born free and equal in dignity and rights;
2. are entitled to all the freedoms in this declaration, regardless of:
   - race
   - color
   - sex
   - language
   - religion
   - political views
   - property
   - or other status;
3. have the right to life, liberty, and security;
4. shall be free from slavery or servitude;
5. must not be subjected to torture or to cruel, inhuman, or degrading treatment or punishment;
6. have the right to recognition as a person before the law;
7. are entitled to equal protection under the law;
8. deserve an effective remedy by a court for acts that violate their fundamental rights;
9. shall be free from arbitrary arrest, detention, or exile;
10. are entitled to a fair and public hearing by an independent, impartial tribunal;
11. have the right to be presumed innocent until proven guilty in court, and shall not be punished for an act that was not considered an offense at the time it was committed;
12. shall be protected from arbitrary interference with their privacy, family, home, or correspondence, and from attacks on their honor;
13. have the right to move freely within their country, and to leave and return to it;

14. may seek and attain asylum from other countries to avoid persecution for political offenses;
15. have the right to a nationality and to change their nationality;
16. retain the right to marry and establish a family, with the free and full consent of both spouses;
17. have the right to own property;
18. may exercise freedom of thought and religion, may change their religion, and may teach or practice their religion publicly or privately;
19. shall have freedom of opinion and expression and may attain information and ideas through any media;
20. have the right to peaceful assembly and association;
21. retain the right to take part in government directly or through chosen representatives, and to vote in genuine and fair elections;
22. have the right to social security and, according to the resources of each nation, to economic, social, and cultural rights that preserve their dignity;
23. have the right to work, to choose their employment, to work in fair and favorable conditions, to receive equal pay for equal work, and to join unions;
24. deserve rest and leisure, including reasonable working hours and periodic paid holidays;
25. have the right to a standard of living adequate for their health and well-being, including food, clothing, housing, medical care, and social services; mothers and children require special assistance;
26. are entitled to a free basic education and equal access to higher education. Education shall promote respect for human rights and tolerance;
27. retain the right to freely share in the cultural life of their community, the arts, and scientific advancements;
28. deserve a social and international order in which the freedoms set forth in this declaration can be fully realized;
29. have duties to the community; freedoms may be limited only when necessary to respect the rights of others and to ensure morality, public order, and general welfare of the society;
30. must not infer any rights from this declaration that would allow a nation, group, or person to perform any act aimed to destroy the freedoms set forth.

According to the United Nations Office of the High Commissioner for Human Rights, human rights are:
- universal and inalienable,
- interdependent and indivisible,
- equal and nondiscriminatory,
- both rights and obligations.

Human Rights in the United States

According to the *World Report 2012* published by Human Rights Watch on the US general human rights record, the following are true:
- In the United States sixteen states have outlawed the death penalty, while thirty-four allow it.
- The number of criminals executed in the United States has been dropping since 2009, when fifty-two were executed.
- Half of all HIV-positive patients in Mississippi are not receiving health care; the risk of dying of AIDS in that state is 60 percent higher than in the rest of the nation.
- In September 2011 a drone strike launched by the United States in Yemen killed American citizen Anwar al-Awlaki. According to President Barack Obama, Awlaki had been al Qaeda's leader of external operations in the Arabian Peninsula, but it was controversial that the United States assassinated an American citizen without affording him due process.
- In October 2011 a drone attack killed Awlaki's sixteen-year-old son and several others. The US government later said his son was not the target.
- US citizen Samir Khan, the editor of an al Qaeda publication, was killed in the same drone strike in September 2011 that killed Awlaki.

Human Rights Across the Globe

The US Bureau of Democracy, Human Rights, and Labor in its *Country Reports on Human Rights Practices for 2011* states the following:

In Cambodia,
- minimum wage for workers in garment factories is about fifty-nine US dollars a month (the poverty level set by the World Bank for Cambodia is about thirty-seven US dollars a month);

- most large factories producing clothing for the United States and other developed countries meet relatively high health and safety standards, but small factories often do not meet such standards;
- in April 2011 about five hundred employees fainted at the Huey Chuen shoe factory; toxic water, fumes, poor nutrition, and panic were the suspected causes; the government provided social security funds to cover their medical care.

In Indonesia,
- around 6 million to 8 million children worked more than three hours a day, the limit set by the government, in clothing work-shops and other industries;
- unions reported that some garment and electronics assembly plants required excessive overtime, which broke the law and jeopardized the health and safety of workers;
- the American Center for International Labor Solidarity found that garment industry workers could not verify that they were compensated for excessive overtime hours because their check stubs did not list the amount of overtime they were paid.

In Vietnam,
- in September 2011 two dozen children were rescued from a private garment factory where they had been forced into slave labor;
- one children's shelter discovered that some underage workers in garment factories were drugged to keep them awake and working longer hours;
- in 2011 the International Labour Organization asserted that sixty-six out of seventy-eight apparel factories did not comply with legal overtime limits.

Opinions on Human Rights Interventions

According to polls conducted by the Pew Research Center's 2012 Global Attitudes Project,
- about one in five respondents believed that promoting human rights in China should be America's most important priority in dealing with that country;
- more than half (53 percent) said that promoting human rights in China is very important—this was an increase from January 2011, when 40 percent thought so;

- the majority of Americans, 62 percent, approved of US drone strikes against extremist leaders in Pakistan and other countries, the only one of the twenty countries surveyed where more people approved them than opposed them;
- in seventeen of twenty countries polled, the majority of respondents opposed US drone attacks, including Greeks (90 percent), Egyptians (89 percent), Jordanians (85 percent), Turks (81 percent), Brazilians (76 percent), Spaniards (76 percent), and Japanese (75 percent).

Organizations to Contact

The editors have compiled the following list of organizations concerned with the issues debated in this book. The descriptions are derived from materials provided by the organizations. All have publications or information available for interested readers. The list was compiled on the date of publication of the present volume; the information provided here may change. Be aware that many organizations take several weeks or longer to respond to inquiries, so allow as much time as possible for the receipt of requested materials.

The Advocates for Human Rights
330 Second Ave. South, Ste. 800
Minneapolis, MN 55401
website: www.theadvocatesforhumanrights.org

This group helps individuals fully realize their human rights in the United States and around the world. For over twenty-five years, the Advocates programs have helped refugees and immigrants, women, ethnic and religious minorities, children, and other marginalized communities whose rights are at risk. The organization has produced seventy-five reports documenting human rights practices in twenty-five countries, many of which are available on its website.

American Civil Liberties Union (ACLU)
125 Broad St., 18th Fl.
New York, NY 10004
(212) 549-2500
website: www.aclu.org

The ACLU is a national organization that works to defend Americans' civil rights guaranteed by the US Constitution. The ACLU publishes and distributes policy statements, pamphlets, newsletters, and reports on various human and civil rights issues.

Amnesty International (AI)
5 Penn Plaza
New York, NY 10001
(212) 807-8400
website: www.amnestyusa.org

AI is a worldwide, independent, voluntary movement that works to free people detained for their beliefs who have not used or advocated violence and people imprisoned because of their ethnic origin, sex, language, national or social origin, economic status, and birth or other status. AI seeks to ensure fair and prompt trials for political prisoners and to abolish torture, "disappearances," cruel treatment of prisoners, and executions. Its website contains links to the numerous reports, brochures, and fact sheets it publishes.

British Institute of Human Rights
School of Law, Queen Mary
University of London
Mile End Rd.
London E1 4NS
United Kingdom
website: www.bihr.org.uk

This British organization is an independent human rights charity committed to challenging inequality and social justice in everyday life in the UK. It holds human rights–related events and seminars and publishes numerous newsletters, policy papers, e-briefings, and reports on a wide range of topics, including health care, immigration, judicial review, and more.

Child Labor Coalition (CLC)
1701 K St. NW, Ste. 1200
Washington, DC 20006
(202) 835-3323
website: www.stopchildlabor.org

The CLC serves as a national network for the exchange of information about child labor. It provides a forum for groups seeking to protect working minors and to end the exploitation of child labor. It works to influence public policy on child labor issues, to protect youths from hazardous work, and to advocate for better enforcement of child labor laws.

European Court of Human Rights
Council of Europe
67075 Strasbourg Cedex
France
+33 (0)3 88 41 20 18
website: www.echr.coe.int/ECHR/Homepage_EN

This international court was set up in 1959. It rules on individual or state applications alleging violations of the civil and political rights set out in the European Convention on Human Rights. Since 1998 it has served as a full-time court, and individuals can apply to it directly. In almost fifty years the court has delivered more than ten thousand judgments and is a powerful living instrument for meeting new challenges and consolidating the rule of law and democracy in Europe. Its website contains numerous human rights–related documents, speeches, court proceedings, and briefs.

Global Exchange
2017 Mission St., No. 303
San Francisco, CA 94110
(800) 497-1994
website: www.globalexchange.org

Global Exchange is a nonprofit organization that promotes social justice, environmental sustainability, and grassroots activism on international human rights issues. Global Exchange produces various books, videos, and other educational programs and materials concerning human rights.

Human Rights First
333 Seventh Ave., 13th Fl.
New York, NY 10001-5108
(212) 845-5200
website: www.humanrightsfirst.org

Human Rights First believes that building respect for human rights and the rule of law will help ensure the dignity to which every individual is entitled and will stem tyranny, extremism, intolerance, and violence. It advocates for change at the highest levels of national and international policy making.

Human Rights in China
450 Seventh Ave., Ste. 1301
New York, NY 10123
(212) 239-4495
website: www.hrichina.org

Founded by Chinese students and scholars in March 1989, Human Rights in China is an international Chinese nongovernmental organization whose mission is to promote international human rights and advance the institutional protection of these rights in the People's Republic of China. It publishes the quarterly journal *China Rights Forum*, and its website contains breaking news reports on events in China.

Human Rights Watch
350 Fifth Ave., 34th Fl.
New York, NY 10118-3299
(212) 290-4700
website: www.hrw.org

Human Rights Watch regularly investigates human rights abuses in over seventy countries around the world. It promotes civil liberties and defends freedom of thought, due process, and equal protection under the law. Its goal is to hold governments accountable for human rights violations that those governments commit against individuals because of the latter's political, ethnic, or religious affiliations. It publishes the *Human Rights Watch Quarterly Newsletter,* the annual *Human Rights Watch World Report,* and a semiannual publications catalog.

International Labour Office (ILO)
4 route des Morillons
CH-1211 Genève 22
Switzerland
website: www.ilo.org

The ILO works to promote basic human rights through improved working and living conditions by enhancing opportunities for those who are excluded from meaningful paid employment. The ILO pioneered such landmarks of industrial society as the eight-hour workday, maternity protection, and workplace safety regulations. It runs the ILO Publications Bureau, which publishes various policy statements and background information on all aspects of employment.

The National Endowment for Democracy (NED)

1101 Fifteenth St. NW, Ste. 700
Washington, DC 20005
(202) 293-9072 • fax: (202) 223-6042
website: www.ned.org

NED is a private, nonprofit organization created in 1983 to strengthen democratic institutions around the world through nongovernmental efforts. It publishes the bimonthly periodical *Journal of Democracy*.

Physicians for Human Rights

2 Arrow St., Ste. 301
Cambridge, MA 02138
(617) 301-4200
website: http://physiciansforhumanrights.org

This group uses medicine and science to prevent mass atrocities and severe human rights violations against individuals. It uses its investigations and expertise to advocate for the prevention of individual or small-scale acts of violence from becoming mass atrocities, the protection of internationally guaranteed rights of individuals and civilian populations, and the prosecution of those who violate human rights. Its website contains numerous reports, papers, videos, and other media on a variety of topics, including rape, asylum, and chemical weapons.

United Nations Human Rights Council

Palais Wilson
52 rue des Pâquis
CH-1201 Geneva
Switzerland
website: www.ohchr.org/EN/HRBodies/HRC/Pages/HRCIndex.aspx

The Human Rights Council is an intergovernmental body within the United Nations system responsible for strengthening the promotion and protection of human rights around the globe and for addressing situations of human rights violations and making recommendations on them. It has the ability to discuss all thematic human rights issues and situations that require its attention throughout the year. It meets at the Geneva offices and is made up of forty-seven member states. The Human Rights Council replaced the United Nations Commission on Human Rights. Its website identifies the rights considered to be human rights and offers numerous papers, briefings, and news updates on a variety of international human rights situations.

For Further Reading

Books

Maude Barlow, *Blue Covenant: The Global Water Crisis and the Coming Battle for the Right to Water.* New York: New Press, 2009. Calls for nations to define the world's freshwater as a human right and a public trust rather than as a commercial product.

Shahzad Bashir and Robert D. Crews, eds., *Under the Drones: Modern Lives in the Afghanistan-Pakistan Borderlands.* Cambridge, MA: Harvard University Press, 2012. Investigates the lives of real people affected by drone strikes and analyzes the political, social, and economic forces that shape their lives.

Medea Benjamin and Barbara Ehrenreich, *Drone Warfare: Killing by Remote Control.* New York: Verso, 2013. A comprehensive analysis of the rise of robot warfare, one of the fastest-growing—and most secretive—fronts in global warfare.

John D. Bessler, *Cruel and Unusual: The American Death Penalty and the Founders' Eighth Amendment.* Southampton, NJ: Northeastern, 2012. Challenges the conventional wisdom that the nation's founders were avid death penalty supporters and shows the founders' conflicting and ambivalent views on capital punishment.

Frank Ching, *China: The Truth About Its Human Rights Record.* E-book. New York: Ebury, 2008. Throws light on the recent history and current status of China's human rights policies and covers issues ranging from the restrictions on speech and worship to the lack of freedom in the judicial, economic, public health, and environmental sectors.

Ronald Deibert, John Palfrey, Rafal Rohozinski, and Jonathan Zittrain, eds., *Access Denied: The Practice and Policy of Global Internet Filtering.* Information Revolution and Global Politics series. Cambridge, MA: MIT Press, 2008. Documents and analyzes Internet filtering practices in more than three dozen countries, offering the first rigorously conducted study of an accelerating trend.

David Garland, *Peculiar Institution: America's Death Penalty in an Age of Abolition*. Cambridge, MA: Belknap Press of Harvard University Press, 2012. Shows how death penalty practice has come to bear the distinctive hallmarks of America's political institutions and cultural conflicts.

Andrea D. Lyon and Alan M. Dershowitz, *Angel of Death Row: My Life as a Death Penalty Defense Lawyer*. New York: Kaplan, 2010. The memoir and experiences of an Illinois death penalty defense lawyer who has tried more than 130 homicide cases.

Matt J. Martin and Charles W. Sasser, *Predator: The Remote-Control Air War over Iraq and Afghanistan; A Pilot's Story*. Minneapolis: Zenith, 2010. Explores how remotely controlled aircraft are killing America's enemies and saving American lives.

Susan L. Shirk, *Changing Media, Changing China*. Oxford: Oxford University Press, 2010. A collection of essays about all aspects of the changing media landscape in China.

Liesbeth Sluiter, *Clean Clothes: A Global Movement to End Sweatshops*. London: Pluto, 2009. Argues that creating conditions for fair labor in the global economy is the greatest moral challenge of our times. Makes multiple suggestions for a sweat-free future.

Periodicals

Morton Abramowitz, "Letting North Korea Starve," *National Interest*, July 5, 2012.

Morton Abramowitz, "Why Is the U.S. Withholding Food Aid from Starving North Korea?," *Atlantic*, July 6, 2012.

Peter Beaumont, "One Year On: Chaotic Libya Reveals the Perils of Humanitarian Intervention," *Guardian* (Manchester, UK), February 19, 2012.www.guardian.co.uk/commentisfree/2012 /feb/19/peter-beaumont-libya-intervention-gaddafi.

Max Boot, "Standing Up for Human Rights in China," *Commentary*, April 29, 2012.

Nathanial Borenstein, "Vint Cerf Is Too Modest; Internet Access Is a Human Right," Mimecast, January 6, 2012. http://blog.mimecast .com/2012/01/vint-cerf-is-too-modest-internet-access-is-a-human -right.

Vinton Cerf, "Internet Access Is Not a Human Right," *New York Times*, January 4, 2012.

Charleston (WV) Gazette, "Health: Care a Human Right," August 5, 2012. http://wvgazette.com/Opinion/Editorials/201208050050.

Suw Charman-Anderson, "The Internet: Not a Human Right, but an Essential Utility," Firstpost, January 7, 2012. www.firstpost.com /tech/the-internet-not-a-human-right-but-an-essential-utility -174677.html.

Dennis Clayson, "Health Care Is in No Way Human Right," *Waterloo–Cedar Falls (IA) Courier*, July 29, 2012. http://wcfcourier .com/news/opinion/clayson/health-care-is-in-no-way-human-right /article_45565df0-d751-11e1-bc22-001a4bcf887a.html.

Jonathan Cook, "The Evils of Humanitarian Wars," Counterpunch, June 26, 2012. www.counterpunch.org/2012/06/26/the-evils-of -humanitarian-wars.

Charles Duhigg and David Barboza, "Apple's iPad and the Human Costs for Workers in China," *New York Times*, January 25, 2012.

Nicholas Eberstadt, "Should North Korea Be Provided with Humanitarian Aid?," American Enterprise Institute, September 22, 2011. www.aei.org/article/should-north-korea-be-provided-with -humanitarian-aid.

Adam Clark Estes, "The Case for (and Against) Internet as a Human Right," *Atlantic*, January 5, 2012.

Frida Ghitis, "On Human Rights, U.S. Must Lead—or No One Will," *Miami (FL) Herald*, August 6, 2012. www.miamiherald .com/2012/08/06/2930361/on-human-rights-us-must-lead-or .html.

Peter H. Gleick, "The Human Right to Water (and Sanitation)," *Huffington Post*, August 4, 2010. www.huffingtonpost.com/peter -h-gleick/the-human-right-to-water_b_671175.html.

Mikhail Gorbachev, "The Right to Water," *New York Times*, July 16, 2010.

Robert Greenberg, "Health Care Should Be a Universal Human Right," *Albuquerque (NM) Journal*, March 13, 2011. www.abq journal.com/opinion/guest columns/1388135289opinionguest columns03-13-11.htm.

Amanda Horner, "Apple Sweatshops in China Unjust," *Northern Arizona News*, April 9, 2012. http://northernarizonanews.com /blog/2012/04/09/apple-sweatshops-in-china-unjust.

Mathew Ingram, "Is Internet Access a Fundamental Human Right?," Gigaom, January 5, 2012. http://gigaom.com/2012/01/05/is-inter net-access-a-fundamental-human-right.

Jeff Jacoby, "What 'Right' to Health Care?," *Boston Globe*, September 13, 2009.

Richard Land, "The Death Penalty Can Be Pro-Life," *Washington Post*, September 15, 2011.

Ewan MacAskill, "Obama: 'I Believe Waterboarding Was Torture, and It Was a Mistake,'" *Guardian* (Manchester, UK), April 29, 2009. www.guardian.co.uk/world/2009/apr/30/obama-water boarding-mistake.

Michelle Martinez, "U.S. Drone Killing of American al-Awlaki Prompts Legal, Moral Debate," CNN.com, September 30, 2011. http://articles.cnn.com/2011-09-30/politics/politics targeting-us-citizens_1_al-awlaki-yemeni-embassy-drone-missile? _s=PM:POLITICS.

Robert Maynard, "Is Healthcare a Human Right?," Renew America, March 27, 2011. www.renewamerica.com/columns/maynard /110327.

Aaron Miller, "The U.S. Shouldn't Intervene in Syria," *Newsday*, August 2, 2012.

Anil Naidoo, "Water Is Now, and Forever, a Human Right," *Epoch Times*, August 7, 2011. www.theepochtimes.com/n2/opinion /water-is-now-and-forever-a-human-right-60072.html.

Andrew Natsios, "U.S. Food Aid to N. Korea Sends the Wrong Messages," *Washington Post*, March 8, 2012.

Kendra Okonski, "Is Water a Human Right?," *New Atlantis*, Spring 2009. www.thenewatlantis.com/publications/is-water-a-human -right.

Michael Payne, "What Audacity! President Obama Lectures China on Human Rights," OpEdnews, January 22, 2011. www.oped news.com/articles/What-Audacity-President-O-by-michael -payne-110121-900.html.

Benjamin Powell, "In Defense of 'Sweatshops,'" Library of Economics and Liberty, June 2, 2008. www.econlib.org/library/Columns /y2008/Powellssweatshops.html.

Robert J.S. Ross, "Hey, Ralph Lauren, Sweatshops Aren't Chic," *Los Angeles Times*, July 19, 2012.

J.D. Rucker, "Internet Access IS a Human Right," Techni.com, January 5, 2012. www.techi.com/2012/01/internet-access-is-a -human-right.

Debra J. Saunders, "Save the Death Penalty," *San Francisco Chronicle*, September 21, 2012.

Dudley Sharp, "Enforcing Penalty Saves Lives," *Atlanta Journal Constitution*, April 25, 2012.

J. Robert Smith, "Do Americans Really Want Humanitarian Wars?," *American Thinker*, April 19, 2011. www.americanthinker .com/2011/04/do_americans_really_want_human.html.

Elizabeth Umlas, "How Apple, Foxconn, and Others Can Address Labor Abuses in Overseas Factories," *Christian Science Monitor*, April 9, 2012.

Adam Wagner, "Is Internet Access a Human Right?," *Guardian* (Manchester, UK), January 11, 2012. www.guardian.co.uk/law/2012 /jan/11/is-internet-access-a-human-right.

David Zetland, "Water Rights and Human Rights," *Forbes*, March 25, 2010.

Websites

Bureau of Justice Statistics Capital Punishment Page (bjs.ojp.us doj.gov/index.cfm?ty=tp&tid=18). Offers excellent statistical information about the death penalty in the United States and contains numerous poll results, statistical analysis, and fact sheets about the death penalty, the executed, and those on death row.

Human Rights Library—University of Minnesota (www1.umn .edu/humanrts). A large collection of international human rights treaties, instruments, general comments, recommendations, decisions, and other documents. Will be helpful to students researching primary sources on human rights.

Living Under Drones (livingunderdrones.org). An anti-drone website that provides first-person testimonials about living near drone warfare.

United Nations: Human Rights (www.un.org/en/rights). Contains fact sheets, news reports, and links about various human rights topics, including human trafficking, child labor, children and armed conflict, and international human rights policies.

The Universal Declaration of Human Rights (www.un.org/en/documents/udhr). Contains the text of this renowned document, the human rights standard for most countries.

US Department of State Human Rights Page (www.state.gov/j/drl/rls/hrrpt). Contains links to the annual Country Reports published by the State Department, which contain authoritative information on the annual state of human rights around the world.

Youth for Human Rights (www.youthforhumanrights.org). The website of a group whose goal is to teach youth about human rights and inspire them to become advocates for tolerance and peace. The site has information about the group's movement and activities and clubs and chapters around the world.

Index

Rwandan genocide (1994), 95

Picture Credits

© ODD ANDERSEN/AFP/GettyImages, 52

© MLADEN ANTONOV/AFP/Getty Images, 11

© Dimas Ardian/Bloomberg/Getty Images, 77

© Ulrich Baumgarten/Getty Images, 111

© LOUAI BESHARA/AFP/Getty Images, 96

© FABRICE COFFRINI/AFP/Getty Images, 81

© Ulrich Doering/Alamy, 25

© Gale/Cengage Learning, 19, 27, 32, 37, 41, 47, 54, 59, 67, 78, 95, 104, 113, 118

© David Grossman/Alamy, 35

© MAHMUD HAMS/AFP/Getty Images, 44

© Katja Heinemann/Aurora Photos/Alamy, 42

© John Moore/Getty Images, 65

© GERRY PENNY/AFP/Getty Images, 103

© Jasjeet Plaha/Hindustan Times/Getty Images, 21

© Ashley Pon/Getty Images, 85

© Alex Segre/Alamy, 13

© Tarko SUDIARNO/AFP/Getty Images, 71

© YOSHIKAZU TSUNO/AFP/Getty Images, 48

© PEDRO UGARTE/AFP/Getty Images, 120

© AMMAD WAHEED/Reuters /Landov, 60

© David White/Alamy, 31

© Andy Wong/AP Images, 90